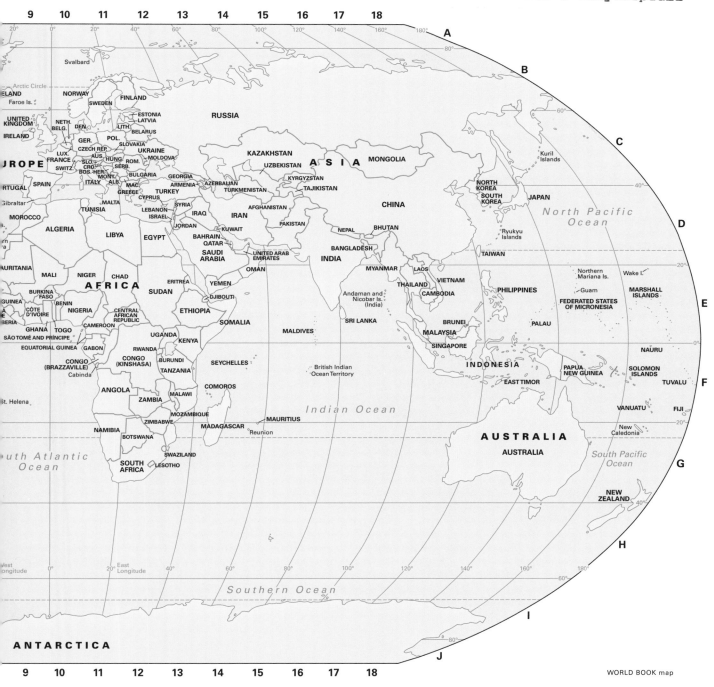

WORLD BOOK map

WORLD BOOK'S
ENCYCLOPEDIA
OF
FLAGS

Volume 10
United States—
Individual States

World Book, Inc.
a Scott Fetzer company
Chicago

Project Consultant: Whitney Smith, Ph.D., Director, Flag Research Center

For information about other World Book publications, visit our
Web site **http://www.worldbook.com** or call **1-800-WORLDBK (967-5325).**
For information about sales to schools and libraries,
call **1-800-975-3250 (United States); 1-800-837-5365 (Canada).**

World Book, Inc.
233 N. Michigan Ave.
Chicago, IL 60601 U.S.A.

Printed in the United States of America

2 3 4 5 6 7 8 9 10 09 08 07 06

**The Library of Congress has cataloged an earlier edition of this title
as follows:**

World Book's encyclopedia of flags.

     p. cm.
  Includes bibliographical references and index.
  ISBN 0-7166-7900-0
  1. Flags. I.Title: Encyclopedia of flags.
CR101.W67 2005
929.9'2'03--dc22

               2005004286

This edition:
ISBN-13: 978-0-7166-7901-1
ISBN-10: 0-7166-7901-9

Additional Resources

Corcoran, Michael. *For Which It Stands.*
  Simon & Schuster, 2002.

Crampton, William G. *Flag.* 1989. Reprint.
  Dorling Kindersley, 2000.

Shearer, Benjamin F. and Barbara S.
  State Names, Seals, Flags, and Symbols. 3rd ed.
  Greenwood, 2001.

Smith, Whitney. *Flag Lore of All Nations.*
  Millbrook, 2001.

Woodcock, Thomas, and Robinson, J.M. *The
  Oxford Guide to Heraldry.* 1988. Reprint.
  Oxford, 1990.

Volume Contents

Set Contents

HOW TO USE THIS SET

World Book's Encyclopedia of Flags contains articles on flags of every nation in the world. The flags are arranged alphabetically, from Afghanistan in Volume 1 to Zimbabwe in Volume 11. The set also includes selected historical flags and flags of organizations and political groups. Volume 12 includes an index for quick access to all entries.

In each of the first 11 volumes, entries for individual countries and their flags are presented on two pages. The first page of each entry contains the country's history and a box listing the nation's capital, head of government, size (in area), major religions, and other important, up-to-date national data. A map in the upper right corner shows the nation's location. Also included on the first page is the history of the nation's flag.

The second page of each entry shows a large color illustration of the national flag and a data box containing key facts about the flag. These facts include a description of the banner and its width-to-length ratio. Certain countries have one flag that is used only by the government, to be flown on public buildings and used for other official purposes (a state flag), and a separate flag for use by private citizens (a civil flag). These instances are noted in the flag data box, and the flag shown will most often be the state flag.

In some volumes, readers will also find state and territory flags for certain countries. Flags of the 50 U.S. states can be found in Volume 10, for example, and flags of the five U.S. territories follow in Volume 11. Volume 11 also contains historical American flags that illustrate the development of the United States from a colony to a modern nation.

1 **Page numbers** are prominently displayed for easy reference.

2 **Entry titles** appear in the colored bar at the top of the page.

3 **Blue disks** at the beginning of entries contain map coordinates keyed to a world map on the endpapers.

4 **Historical information** about the nation, state, or territory provides important background material.

5 **Flag histories** explain how the banner was created.

6 **Locator maps** show the location of a place within its region.

7 **Data boxes** contain easy-to-access facts.

8 **Flags** of each country are shown in large size.

9 **Flag data boxes** include a description of the banner and its width-to-length ratio.

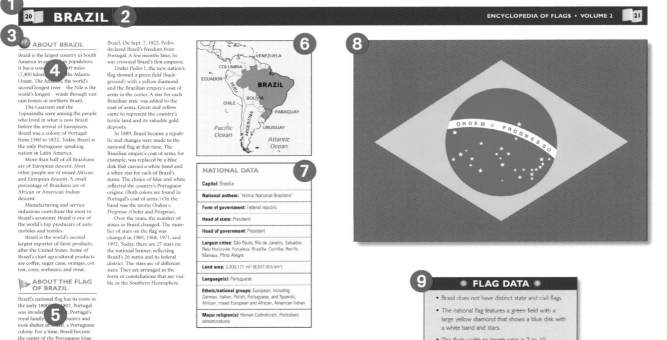

THE PARTS OF A FLAG

Special terms are sometimes used when discussing a flag. The flag's background, for example, is known as the *field*. The field is almost always a single color.

The part of the flag closest to the staff is known as the *hoist*. This is the side of the flag that is hoisted up the flagstaff. The free end of a flag, farthest from the staff, is called the *fly*. Some nations add a *badge*, or emblem, on the fly end of their banner.

The upper corner of a flag, next to the staff, is called the *canton*. Some nations and organizations include a symbol or badge in the cantons of their flags. For example, the banners of nations or other areas that were once part of the United Kingdom often include the British flag, the Union Jack, in the canton, as does this provincial flag of Ontario that is shown at right.

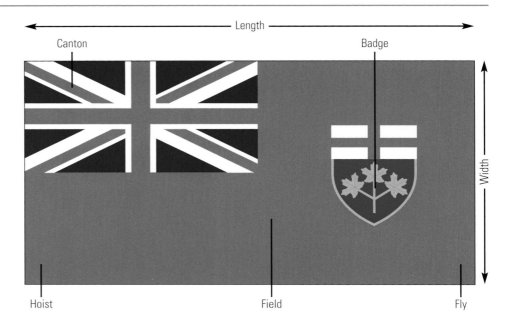

FLAG SHAPES

Flags come in different shapes and sizes. Most national banners—such as the flag of Mexico (upper left) are *rectangular* in shape and are flown horizontally (with the longest part of the banner running from left to right). Some flags have unusual shapes, however. Switzerland's flag (bottom left) is *square*. The flag of the U.S. state of Ohio (upper right) is *swallow-tailed* (forked at the fly end). The example from the International Alphabet flags (bottom right) is *pennant-shaped*.

Rectangle

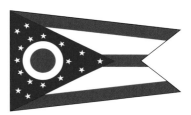

Swallow-tailed

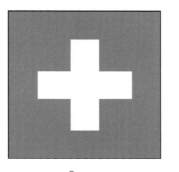

Square

Pennant

RAISING THE FLAG

To raise a flag, the banner is first attached to the halyard, the rope that runs up to the top of the flagstaff. One end of the halyard is attached to the upper corner of the flag's hoist, while the other end is attached to the lower corner of the flag's hoist. The banner is then raised to the top of the staff by pulling on the lower end of the halyard. The flag of the United States should be raised quickly and lowered slowly. It should never be allowed to touch the ground.

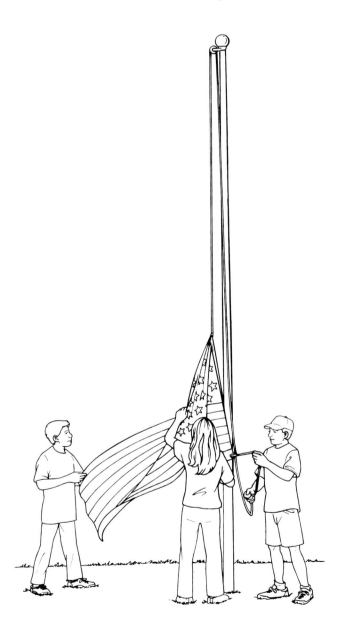

HERALDRY

Many national flags in use today were influenced by *heraldry*. Heraldry is the study of the symbols and designs used on coats of arms, flags, seals, and the like, which are used to represent families, countries, and institutions. The most important heraldic symbol is the coat of arms. Coats of arms were first used on the shields of knights. These unique symbols helped the knight's followers recognize him in battle. Today, many modern flags include a distinct coat of arms.

Over time, heraldry developed a language all its own. Shield and arms colors were called by certain names, such as *purpure*, an Old English word for purple. Certain symbols came to carry special meaning. A crescent, for example, represented a second son, while a rose represented a seventh son.

Although many nations have abolished heraldry because of its connection to social status and privilege, heraldic influences are still evident on flags today. For example, Mexico's flag follows the heraldic practice of separating two colors by a white or yellow line.

This shield shows a *saltire* (diagonal cross)—a design that appears in a number of modern flags.

The standard of Sir Henry Stafford, from around 1475. The cross of St. George at the hoist identifies this as English.

KEY TO COLOR BARS

Each flag entry is bordered by a color-coded bar that allows readers to quickly identify the type of flag being covered. Blue bars represent national flags, while red bars symbolize states, provinces, or internal territories. Teal bars denote certain types of territories, including overseas territories, autonomous regions, and dependencies. Certain regions are, however, represented by a green bar. In addition, green bars are used to denote historical flags that were important in past times or flags that have influenced the development of modern flags. Purple bars represent banners used by international organizations.

NATIONS

STATES, PROVINCES, TERRITORIES

DEPENDENCIES, REGIONS

HISTORICAL

INTERNATIONAL ORGANIZATIONS

C4 ABOUT THE UNITED STATES

The United States is a country that occupies middle North America and includes Alaska in northwestern North America and Hawaii in the Pacific Ocean. The geography of the mainland varies greatly. Coastal lowlands run from the northeast to the south. Mountains and valleys make up the eastern interior. Vast central plains provide farmland. Mountains, canyons, deserts, and valleys cover much of the west.

The ancestors of American Indians crossed from Asia to North America at least 15,000 years ago. About 1 million Indians lived in North America when Europeans arrived in the 1500's. In the 1600's, British colonists settled along the East Coast. The colonies won independence from Britain in 1783.

The population expanded westward throughout the 1800's, displacing native peoples. The Northern and Southern states fought a war between 1861 and 1865 over slavery, which was outlawed at the war's end. The international influence of the United States expanded with its involvement in World War I (1914–1918) and World War II (1939–1945).

Today's U.S. population includes both new immigrants and descendants of people from countries the world over. Most African Americans are descendants of Africans brought to the country as slaves. The U.S. economy is the world's largest. Service industries make up the largest part of the economy.

 ABOUT THE FLAG OF THE UNITED STATES

After the start of the American Revolution (1775–1783), the first unofficial U.S. flag was raised in Massachusetts on Jan. 1, 1776. Known as the Continental Colors, the flag had 13 horizontal stripes, probably red and white or red, white, and blue, representing the 13 colonies. The *canton* (the upper corner of a flag, next to the staff) carried the Union Jack, Great Britain's national flag. The first official national flag, the Stars and Stripes, was approved by the Continental Congress on June 14, 1777. The flag included a blue canton with 13 stars.

The Stars and Stripes changed on May 1, 1795, after the admission of Vermont (1791) and Kentucky (1792) to the Union. At that time, two more stars and two more stripes were added. In 1818, after five more states joined the Union, Congress passed a law stating that the number of stripes should be changed back to, and always remain at, 13. The law also required a new star, representing each new state, to be added on the July 4 after the state's admission. This has been the system ever since. In 1912, an executive order made the flag's design standard. In 1934, the exact shades of color were made standard.

The 50 stars stand for the 50 states of the Union, and the 13 stripes stand for the original 13 states. There is no official meaning or symbolism to the colors of the flag. However, the meaning of the colors in the Great Seal, the national symbol of the United States, was given in a report made by Charles Thomson to Congress in 1782. In this report, Thomson, the secretary of the Congress and the person who prepared the design used on the face of the Great Seal, said: "White signifies purity and innocence, Red, hardiness and valor, and Blue … signifies vigilance, perseverance and justice."

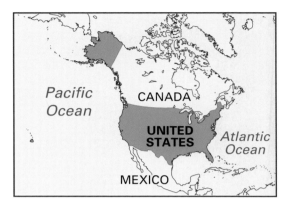

NATIONAL DATA

Capital: Washington, D.C.

National anthem: "The Star-Spangled Banner"

National motto: *In God We Trust*

Form of government: Republic

Head of state: President

Head of government: President

Largest cities: New York City, Los Angeles, Chicago, Houston, Philadelphia, Phoenix, San Diego, Dallas

Land area: 3,615,276 mi² (9,363,520 km²), including 78,937 mi² (204,447 km²) of inland water, but excluding 60,053 mi² (155,535 km²) of Great Lakes and Lake St. Clair and 42,529 mi² (110,148 km²) of coastal water

Language(s): English is the chief language, followed by Spanish.

Ethnic/national groups: Whites, people of Hispanic origin (who may also be white, black, or American Indian), blacks, people of Asian descent, American Indians

Major religion(s): Protestantism, Roman Catholicism, Eastern Orthodoxy, Judaism, Mormonism, Islam

☀ FLAG DATA ☀

- The United States does not have distinct state and civil flags.

- The national flag features 50 white stars on a blue canton with a field of 13 alternating stripes of equal width—7 red and 6 white.

- The flag's width-to-length ratio is 10 to 19.

ABOUT ALABAMA

Alabama is a state in the southern United States. Its name comes from *Alibamu*, the name of an Indian tribe that lived in the area.

Alabama's land ranges from plains in the south to low mountains in the northeast. The state has 53 miles (85 kilometers) of coastline along the Gulf of Mexico.

Indians lived in Alabama from about 8,000 years ago. Spanish explorers arrived in the 1500's. The French colonized the area in the early 1700's. The U.S. admitted Alabama as a slave state (a state that permitted slavery) in 1819.

Alabama *seceded* (withdrew) from the Union in 1861 because of disagreements with the federal government about slavery. After the Civil War (1861–1865), the state was readmitted in 1868. In the mid-1900's, events important in the Civil Rights movement occurred in Alabama.

People of European ancestry make up the majority of Alabama's population. About a fourth of the state's people are African Americans. There are also a number of American Indians.

Alabama's economy is based on the manufacturing of such goods as industrial chemicals and paper products. Other important economic activities include farming, mining, and service industries.

ABOUT THE FLAG OF ALABAMA

During the Civil War, an unofficial flag of blue with a yellow or white star represented Alabama after it separated from the Union. Another blue flag flew over the state capitol. The flag's *obverse* side (the side of a coin, medal, flag, or the like, that features the principal design)

showed the state seal with the goddess Liberty holding a sword and the unofficial flag. The *reverse* (back) side showed a cotton plant and a coiled rattlesnake.

After the Civil War, many citizens wanted to create a new flag. The design chosen in 1895 was a white flag with a red *saltire* (diagonal cross). The flag law referred to the design as a "cross of St. Andrew." However, the cross of St. Andrew, as used by Scotland, has always been described as a white saltire.

No explanation of the flag's symbolism was given. However, the intent of the designer was clear. The flag's square shape was a subtle reminder of the Battle Flag of the Confederate States of America. In 1905, the Alabama legislature considered a proposal to add stars to the state flag. This change would have made it even more similar to the Confederate Battle Flag. However, the change was rejected. A 1985 decision by the state's Supreme Court determined the official flag would be rectangular in shape.

In 1939, Alabama adopted a state coat of arms that used the Confederate Battle Flag, along with the flags of other governments that had controlled Alabama: France, Spain, and Great Britain.

In 1939, Alabama readopted its original state shield, which showed a map of Alabama and its rivers. The shield replaced one that had been designed by Alabama's government after the Civil War. That shield featured the U.S. shield and bald eagle.

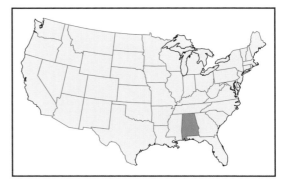

STATE DATA

Popular name: The Heart of Dixie

Capital: Montgomery

Song: "Alabama"

Motto: *Audemus Jura Nostra Defendere* (We Dare Defend Our Rights)

Bird: Yellowhammer

Flower: Camellia

Tree: Southern longleaf pine

Executive: Governor

Largest cities: Birmingham, Montgomery, Mobile, Huntsville, Tuscaloosa, Hoover

Land area: 51,718 mi^2 (133,950 km^2), including 968 mi^2 (2,507 km^2) of inland water, but excluding 519 mi^2 (1,343 km^2) of coastal water

✹ FLAG DATA ✹

- The state flag of Alabama features a white field with a red saltire.

- The most common width-to-length ratios for the flag are 2 to 3, 3 to 5, and 5 to 8.

B2 ABOUT ALASKA

Alaska forms North America's northwestern corner and is the largest U.S. state in area. Alaska claims North America's highest mountain (Mount McKinley—20,320 feet, or 6,194 meters) and biggest glacier (Malaspina—50 miles, or 80 kilometers, wide).

Alaska has two large mountain regions: the Pacific Mountain System in southern Alaska and the Brooks Range in the north. Between the mountain ranges is a large area of low hills and wide valleys. Along the Arctic coast is a frigid plain. The Aleutian Island chain extends 1,100 miles (1,800 kilometers) west of the mainland.

People probably first entered the area now known as Alaska from Asia at least 15,000 years ago. Europeans reached the area in the 1700's, encountering Inuit, Aleuts, and Indians, whose descendants still live there. Russians established the first white settlement in the area in 1784. The United States purchased the region in 1867.

Oil drilled in the Arctic north brings wealth to Alaska. Service industries provide the most jobs. Other important activities include tourism and fishing.

ABOUT THE FLAG OF ALASKA

The territories of the United States usually did not have flags of their own before becoming states. Alaska is an exception. In 1926, the American Legion sponsored a competition to find a distinct territorial flag for Alaska. The following year, Alaska's legislature approved the winning design, which remained unchanged when the territory became a state in 1959.

The winner of the design competition was Benny Benson, a 13-year-old boy living in an orphanage. Benson chose straightforward symbols that appealed to Alaskans of all ages and backgrounds. The flag's dark blue *field* (background) symbolizes the Alaskan sky and the forget-me-not flowers that grow throughout Alaska in the springtime. The North Star—shown in the top corner of the *fly* (the free end of a flag, farthest from the staff)—is an appropriate symbol for Alaska because Alaska is the northernmost state of the United States. The two states that were previously the northernmost states before Alaska—Minnesota and Maine—also show the North Star in their flags.

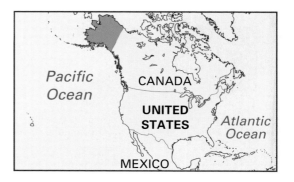

STATE DATA

Popular name: The Last Frontier

Capital: Juneau

Song: "Alaska's Flag"

Motto: *North to the Future*

Bird: Willow ptarmigan

Flower: Forget-me-not

Tree: Sitka spruce

Executive: Governor

Largest cities: Anchorage, Juneau, Fairbanks, College, Sitka, Ketchikan

Land area: 587,878 mi² (1,522,596 km²), including 17,502 mi² (45,329 km²) of inland water, but excluding 27,355 mi² (70,848 km²) of coastal water

✴ FLAG DATA ✴

- The state flag of Alaska features a dark blue field with stars in gold or yellow. The stars represented are Polaris (the North Star) and the Big Dipper, seven stars that form part of the Ursa Major (Great Bear) constellation.

- The flag's width-to-length ratio is 125 to 177.

ABOUT ARIZONA

Arizona is a state in the southwestern United States. Two large land regions, separated by a narrow mountainous area, make up the state. The Colorado Plateau, in the north, includes the Grand Canyon of the Colorado River, Monument Valley, and the Painted Desert. In the south is the Basin and Range Region. It includes mountains, dry but fertile valleys, deserts, and most of Arizona's cities.

Long before Europeans came to what is now Arizona, Indians settled there and established civilizations called the Anasazi, Hohokam, and Mogollon. In the 1600's and 1700's, Spaniards gradually took over the region. The United States acquired most of Arizona's land in 1848 following a war with Mexico. Mexico had received the area, along with its independence, from Spain in the 1820's.

Arizona has large Hispanic and American Indian minorities as well as people of many other ethnic backgrounds. Most employment is in service industries, though tourism, mining, and agriculture are also important. Farming in Arizona generally requires irrigation.

ABOUT THE FLAG OF ARIZONA

On February 27, 1917, five years after becoming a U.S. state, Arizona adopted its state flag. Unlike many other state flags, which were based on military colors or other banners flown during the Civil War (1861–1865), Arizona's design was inspired by the state's natural setting. The rays above the dark blue stripe suggest a colorful Arizona sunset over a desert in shadow. The central star symbolizes the copper found in the state. (The star is supposed to be shown in a metallic-copper color, but is usually shown in an orange-tan shade.) The red and yellow colors are from the Spanish flag, referring to the early European explorers of the area. That red and the blue on the flag are the same as those in the Stars and Stripes, representing American patriotism.

Charles W. Harris, an officer in the Arizona National Guard, designed the flag. The first copy was sewn by Nancy Hayden, the wife of Carl Hayden, who served Arizona in the U.S. Congress for 56 years. Before the flag was adopted in 1917, it was carried by the Arizona National Guard rifle team during a trip to Ohio.

STATE DATA

Popular name: The Grand Canyon State

Capital: Phoenix

Songs: "Arizona March Song" and "Arizona"

Motto: *Ditat Deus* (God Enriches)

Bird: Cactus wren

Flower: Saguaro cactus blossom

Tree: Paloverde

Executive: Governor

Largest cities: Phoenix, Tucson, Mesa, Glendale, Scottsdale, Chandler

Land area: 114,007 mi^2 (295,276 km^2), including 364 mi^2 (943 km^2) of inland water

☀ FLAG DATA ☀

- The state flag of Arizona features red and yellow rays extending from a copper-colored star, above a horizontal blue stripe.

- The flag's width-to-length ratio is 2 to 3.

ABOUT ARKANSAS

Arkansas is a state in the southern United States. Its name comes from an Indian word meaning *downstream people.*

Mountains, forests, and grazing land cover northern and western Arkansas. Fertile lowlands lie along the Mississippi River, which forms most of the state's eastern border. Southern Arkansas is mostly flat.

Indians lived in what is now Arkansas about 12,000 years ago. In the 1700's, control of the area alternated between France and Spain. The United States acquired it as part of the Louisiana Purchase in 1803 and admitted Arkansas as a slave state (a state that permitted slavery) in 1836.

Arkansas *seceded* (withdrew) from the Union in 1861 because of disagreements with the federal government about slavery. After the Civil War (1861–1865), the state was readmitted in 1868. Arkansas became a focus of the Civil Rights movement in 1957, when federal troops enforced the right of black students to attend a high school in Little Rock.

People of European ancestry make up the majority of the state's population. Leading minority groups include African Americans and American Indians.

Arkansas leads the United States in rice farming and ranks high in chicken production. Service industries employ the most people.

ABOUT THE FLAG OF ARKANSAS

In 1911, the Arkansas legislature failed to approve a flag proposal made by the Federation of Women's Clubs. Two years later, the Arkansas secretary of state set up a committee to select an appropriate state flag. Of the 65 designs submitted to the committee, one created by Miss Willie K. Hocker, a member of the Daughters of the American Revolution, was selected. Arkansas's legislature voted to accept this design, and a copy was presented to the battleship U.S.S. *Arkansas.*

The three stars that originally appeared in the center of the flag recalled that Arkansas was the third state created from the Louisiana Territory and that it had been ruled by three different countries (France, Spain, and the United States). The flag was altered in 1923, when a fourth star was added to stand for the Confederate States of America. The banner's final form was approved on April 10, 1924. The colors of Arkansas's flag are the same as those of the U.S. flag. The shape of the central emblem symbolizes Arkansas's status as the only diamond-producing state in the nation. And the 25 stars on the diamond border represent the state's status as the 25th to join the Union.

STATE DATA

Popular name: The Natural State

Capital: Little Rock

Song: "Arkansas"

Motto: *Regnat Populus* (The People Rule)

Bird: Mockingbird

Flower: Apple blossom

Tree: Pine tree

Executive: Governor

Largest cities: Little Rock, Fort Smith, North Little Rock, Fayetteville, Jonesboro, Pine Bluff

Land area: 53,183 mi^2 (137,742 km^2), including 1,107 mi^2 (2,867 km^2) of inland water

※ FLAG DATA ※

- The state flag of Arkansas features a red *field* (background) with a blue and white design. The center of the design is a white diamond with four stars and the name of the state in blue. Surrounding the diamond is a blue band with 25 white stars.

- The most common width-to-length ratios for the flag are 2 to 3, 3 to 5, and 5 to 8.

ⓒ4 ABOUT CALIFORNIA

California is a West Coast state of the United States. It has the largest population and the largest economy of any U.S. state.

The Sierra Nevada mountains cover much of eastern California. Mountains also rise along its northern Pacific Ocean coast. Between the mountain ranges is the immense, fertile Central Valley. Deserts occupy much of the southeast.

Numerous Indians were living in the region when Spaniards first visited in 1542. Starting in 1697, the Spaniards began establishing settlements and missions. The area became a Mexican province in 1822.

People from the United States—the border of which was then far to the east—poured into California during an 1848 gold rush. The United States obtained the land that same year after a war with Mexico.

Three-quarters of today's Californians were born in the United States. The state has large communities of Native Americans and people from Latin America and Asia.

California produces more manufactured goods and food than any other state. Its economy also has a large service sector. California is a world center of motion-picture and television production.

▷ ABOUT THE FLAG OF CALIFORNIA

The Bear Flag Revolt occurred during the Mexican-American War (1846–1848). On June 14, 1846, a group of American settlers in the Mexican-ruled territory of California declared their independence from Mexico and hoisted the original Bear Flag. The following month, U.S. naval forces seized control of the area. As a result, the flag of the short-lived California Republic was replaced by the Stars and Stripes.

The memory of the Bear Flag was kept alive, however, even though original examples of the banner were lost or destroyed. In 1911, the California legislature recognized the Bear Flag as the official state flag. The California grizzly bear, shown as the central emblem, is now extinct. The California flag, like those of Hawaii and Texas, is unusual in that it features a design used by a formerly independent country.

STATE DATA

Popular name: The Golden State

Capital: Sacramento

Song: "I Love You, California"

Motto: *Eureka* (I Have Found It)

Bird: California valley quail

Flower: Golden poppy

Tree: California redwood

Executive: Governor

Largest cities: Los Angeles, San Diego, San Jose, San Francisco, Long Beach, Fresno

Land area: 158,648 mi² (410,896 km²), including 2,674 mi² (6,925 km²) of inland water, but excluding 222 mi² (574 km²) of Pacific coastal water

🌟 FLAG DATA 🌟

- The state flag of California features a white *field* (background) with a California grizzly bear above the words *California Republic* and a red stripe. In the upper corner of the *hoist* (the part of the flag closest to the staff) is a single red star.

- The flag's width-to-length ratio is 2 to 3.

C4 ABOUT COLORADO

Colorado is a state in the west-central United States. It is named for the Colorado River, which rises in the state. Spanish explorers called the river *colorado*—meaning *colored red*—because of its red-stone canyons.

The North American Great Plains cover the eastern two-fifths of Colorado. This mostly flat region contrasts sharply with the central section of the state, which includes mountain peaks, plateaus, and deep valleys. Hills, plateaus, and valleys cover the western area.

The Anasazi, an Indian people, built cliff dwellings in parts of what is now Colorado long before Europeans arrived in the 1600's. The United States acquired part of Colorado in the 1803 Louisiana Purchase and the remainder in 1848. The region remained sparsely settled until mining booms in the late 1800's. The state's economy expanded greatly during World War II (1939–1945).

Most of Colorado's growing number of people live in cities along the western edge of the Great Plains. Service industries, especially tourism, make up the largest part of Colorado's economy. High-tech industries are also important.

ABOUT THE FLAG OF COLORADO

Like many of the Western States, Colorado has an easily recognizable design for its flag. The *C* stands for the name of the state. The letter's color also recalls the origin of the state's name. The *C* also stands for the state flower, the columbine, and the state nickname, the *Centennial State*. This nickname was chosen because Colorado became a state in 1876, 100 years after the United States became independent.

The red, white, and blue of the U.S. flag are all colors that appear in the Colorado flag, as are the blue, yellow, and white of the columbine. The flag colors represent the blue sky, the yellow sun, and the white of mountain snows. The yellow and white of the flag also reflect the area's many deposits of gold and silver. Gold and silver brought many early settlers to the territory, and these minerals are still mined in Colorado today. The original flag design was approved in 1911. The flag took its present form on March 31, 1964, when the *C* was enlarged and the central yellow disk made the same size as the white stripe.

STATE DATA

Popular name: The Centennial State

Capital: Denver

Song: "Where the Columbines Grow"

Motto: *Nil sine Numine* (Nothing Without Providence)

Bird: Lark bunting

Flower: White and lavender columbine

Tree: Colorado blue spruce

Executive: Governor

Largest cities: Denver, Colorado Springs, Aurora, Lakewood, Fort Collins, Arvada

Land area: 104,100 mi² (269,618 km²), including 371 mi² (960 km²) of inland water

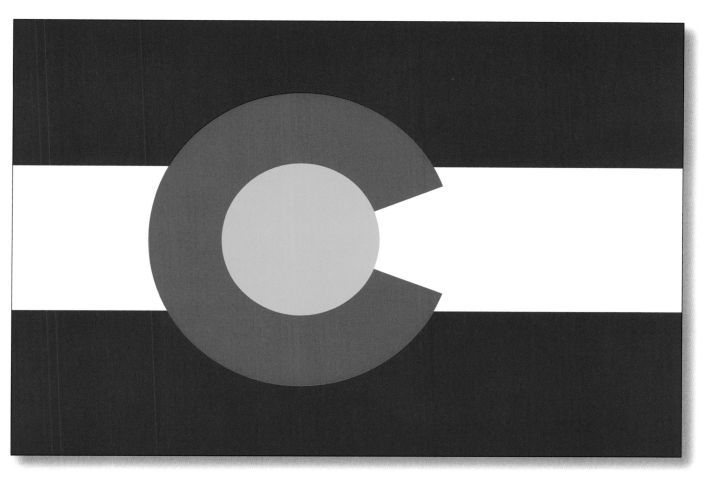

☀ FLAG DATA ☀

- The state flag of Colorado features three horizontal stripes of equal width—blue, white, and blue—with a red C surrounding a yellow (or gold) disk.

- The width-to-length ratios of the flag are 10 to 19, 2 to 3, and 3 to 5, depending on where it is being displayed.

C4 ABOUT CONNECTICUT

Connecticut is a state in the northeastern United States. Its name comes from an Algonquian Indian word meaning *on the long tidal river,* referring to what is now known as the Connecticut River, which flows through the center of the state.

Eastern and northwestern uplands frame the Connecticut River Valley. Lowlands line the coast, 618 miles (955 kilometers) along Long Island Sound.

Several Algonquian Indian tribes were living in what is now Connecticut when Europeans arrived after 1600. English colonists from Massachusetts established the first permanent white settlement in 1633. People from Connecticut had important roles during the American Revolution and the early years of independence. In 1788, Connecticut became the fifth state to *ratify* (approve) the U.S. Constitution.

People of Italian, Irish, English, German, and Polish descent constitute the state's largest population groups. Hispanic Americans and African Americans each account for about a tenth of the population.

Manufacturing and service industries, including finance, insurance, and tourism, make up most of Connecticut's economy. The state is a leading U.S. producer of helicopters and submarines.

ABOUT THE FLAG OF CONNECTICUT

The coat of arms that appears on Connecticut's flag is based on the 1711 seal of the colony of Connecticut. Its three grapevines may represent Connecticut, New Haven, and Saybrook, three separate colonies that eventually combined to create Connecticut. Or they may symbolize the first three towns established by Europeans: Hartford, Wethersfield, and Windsor. Below the shield is an inscription in Latin: *Qui Transtulit Sustinet* (He Who Transplanted Still Sustains). This motto may refer to the 80th Psalm of the Bible, which contains the text: "Thou hast brought a vine out of Egypt …"

The basic design of the flag flown today was first used during the American Revolution (1775–1783). At that time, however, the color of the *field* (background) varied. Each Connecticut regiment had its own color. During the Civil War (1861–1865), blue was the standard field color of flags flown by regiments from Connecticut and other Union states. Many Connecticut residents began thinking of those military flags as representing their state. As a result, a flag with a blue field was later flown over the state capitol when the legislature was in session. That flag served as the basis for the current banner, adopted in June 1897.

STATE DATA

Popular name: The Constitution State

Capital: Hartford

Song: "Yankee Doodle"

Motto: *Qui Transtulit Sustinet* (He Who Transplanted Still Sustains)

Bird: American robin

Flower: Mountain laurel

Tree: White oak

Executive: Governor

Largest cities: Bridgeport, New Haven, Hartford, Stamford, Waterbury, Norwalk

Land area: 5,006 mi^2 (12,966 km^2), including 161 mi^2 (416 km^2) of inland water, but excluding 538 mi^2 (1,392 km^2) of coastal water

✴ FLAG DATA ✴

- The state flag of Connecticut features a blue field with a central coat of arms showing three grapevines. A ribbon below the arms bears an inscription in Latin.

- The flag's width-to-length ratio is 26 to 33.

DELAWARE

ABOUT DELAWARE

Delaware is a state on the East Coast of the United States. It takes its name from Delaware Bay, the body of water that an English sea captain named *De La Warr Bay* in 1610 for Lord De La Warr (1577–1618), governor of Virginia. Most of Delaware is a coastal plain. The northern edge has hills and valleys.

Algonquian Indians lived in present-day Delaware when English explorer Henry Hudson (?–1611) sailed into its bay in 1609. Swedes founded the first permanent settlement in 1638, which eventually fell under Dutch, then English, control. In 1682, James, Duke of York (1633–1701), made the Delaware area a territory of the Pennsylvania colony, to which it remained attached until 1776. Delaware was the first state to *ratify* (approve) the U.S. Constitution.

About one-fifth of Delaware's population is African American. Descendants of Irish, German, English, and Italian immigrants make up other large population groups.

About 200,000 companies are incorporated in Delaware because of its favorable business laws. Chemicals are the state's primary manufactured product.

ABOUT THE FLAG OF DELAWARE

During the Revolutionary War (1775–1783), troops from Delaware carried their own distinct banners. However, an official state flag was not adopted until July 24, 1913. The diamond shape shown on the state's flag is a reminder of an early nickname for Delaware, the *Diamond State*. Some historians believe Delaware received that nickname because, though it was small in size, it was valuable for its location on the Atlantic Ocean. The flag's colors, colonial blue and buff (or light tan), were chosen because they matched the uniform of General George Washington, who led the Continental Army.

The date along the bottom of the flag is the day that Delaware became the first state to ratify the U.S. Constitution. The coat of arms, which also appears in the state seal, was approved in 1777. It features symbols that were appropriate for Delaware in the late 1700's: a soldier, a farmer, a sheaf of wheat, an ear of corn, an ox, and a ship. Beneath these symbols is the state motto, *Liberty and Independence*.

STATE DATA

Popular name: The First State

Capital: Dover

Song: "Our Delaware"

Motto: *Liberty and Independence*

Bird: Blue hen chicken

Flower: Peach blossom

Tree: American holly

Executive: Governor

Largest cities: Wilmington, Dover, Newark, Pike Creek, Bear, Brookside

Land area: 2,026 mi^2 (5,246 km^2), including 71 mi^2 (184 km^2) of inland water, but excluding 371 mi^2 (960 km^2) of coastal water

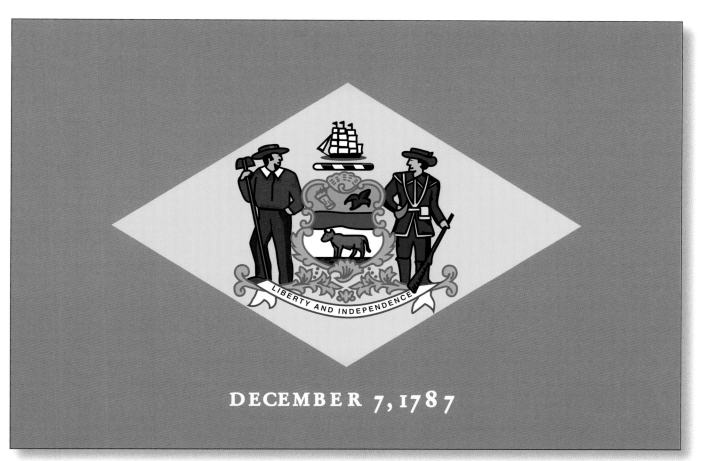

※ FLAG DATA ※

- The state flag of Delaware features a blue *field* (background) with a buff, or light tan, diamond. The diamond bears a central coat of arms above the inscription *December 7, 1787*, the date on which Delaware ratified the U.S. Constitution.

- The most common width-to-length ratios for the flag are 2 to 3, 3 to 5, and 5 to 8.

C4 ABOUT FLORIDA

Florida is the southernmost state in the mainland United States. Florida consists of a long peninsula between the Gulf of Mexico and the Atlantic Ocean and a chain of islands off its southern tip. Coastal plains cover much of the mainland. A region of more elevated land, called the Florida uplands, lies in the north and center.

Indians inhabited present-day Florida 12,000 years ago. In 1565, on the eastern coast, Spaniards founded St. Augustine, the first permanent European settlement in what is now the United States. During the 1600's and 1700's, the Spanish and English competed for Florida, until it came under U.S. control in 1821. Florida was admitted to the Union as a slave state (a state that permitted slavery) in 1845. Florida *seceded* (withdrew) from the Union in 1861 because of disagreements with the federal government about slavery. After the Civil War (1861-1865), the state was readmitted in 1868.

Florida's population has grown rapidly since the mid-1900's. Most Floridians live in cities. Florida has large African American and Hispanic American minorities. Florida's economy includes tourism, agriculture, high-technology manufacturing, and service industries.

ABOUT THE FLAG OF FLORIDA

The first flag of Florida was raised on June 25, 1845, at the inauguration of William D. Moseley, the state's first governor. That first flag had five horizontal stripes of blue, orange, red, white, and green, and a ribbon that bore the words *Let Us Alone*. The U.S. flag appeared in the banner's *canton* (the upper corner of the flag, next to the staff). The symbolism of the colors is not known. The motto, however, reflects the state's desire to preserve its own rights and its distaste for a strong federal government. The banner was rarely used.

The next state flag was adopted on Jan. 13, 1861, after Florida seceded from the Union. The design was similar in many ways to the Stars and Stripes. It had 13 horizontal stripes—red and white—with a white star on a blue canton. The banner was approved by the commander of Florida's armed forces. The next flag, adopted on Sept. 13, 1861, was based on the Stars and Bars of the Confederate States of America. It had red, white, and red horizontal stripes and a vertical blue stripe that carried an elaborate seal.

After the Civil War, Florida adopted a new flag. On Aug. 6, 1868, the state seal was placed in the center of a white flag. The seal's design showed an American Indian woman standing on a piece of land jutting into water, where a steamboat sailed. A band with the state name and the motto *In God We Trust* completed the design. On Nov. 6, 1900, a red *saltire* (diagonal cross) was added to the white *field* (background) so the banner would not resemble a symbol of surrender. The design may also have been based on the saltire in the Confederate Battle Flag. On May 21, 1985, the state seal was revised to change such elements as the tribe of the Indian woman depicted on the seal and the type of palm tree.

STATE DATA

Popular name: The Sunshine State

Capital: Tallahassee

Song: "Old Folks at Home" ("Swanee River")

Motto: *In God We Trust* (unofficial)

Bird: Mockingbird

Flower: Orange blossom

Tree: Sabal palm

Executive: Governor

Largest cities: Jacksonville, Miami, Tampa, St. Petersburg, Hialeah, Orlando

Land area: 58,681 mi² (151,982 km²), including 4,683 mi² (12,129 km²) of inland water, but excluding 1,308 mi² (3,388 km²) of coastal water

✳ FLAG DATA ✳

- The state flag of Florida features a white field with a red saltire. The state seal is displayed in the flag's center.

- The width-to-length ratios for the flag are 2 to 3, 3 to 5, and 5 to 8.

C4 ABOUT GEORGIA

Georgia is a state in the southern United States. It was named for King George II (1683–1760) of England.

Landforms in northern Georgia include mountains and the hilly Piedmont. Flat coastal plains cover the southern half of the state.

Indians had lived in the region for thousands of years before Spanish settlers and English colonists arrived in the 1500's and 1600's. English colonists led by James Oglethorpe (1696–1785) settled Savannah in 1733. Oglethorpe promoted economic equality in the colony, but settlement was eventually opened to planters using slave labor. Georgia became a U.S. state in 1788.

Georgia *seceded* (withdrew) from the Union in 1861 because of disagreements with the federal government about slavery. During the Civil War (1861–1865), Georgia suffered much destruction from Union armies. Georgia rejoined the Union in 1870.

People of European ancestry make up the majority of Georgia's population. Nearly a third of the population is African American.

Georgia's farms produce cotton, peanuts, tobacco, and peaches. Factories make such products as processed foods, chemicals, and textiles. Service industries provide the largest proportion of Georgia's income.

ABOUT THE FLAG OF GEORGIA

Georgia's first official state flag was established on Oct. 17, 1879. Like the Stars and Bars flag of the Confederate States of America, Georgia's banner had three equal stripes of red, white, and red. Instead of a design in the *canton* (the upper corner of the flag, next to the staff), however, the state flag had a vertical blue stripe along the *hoist* (the part of the flag closest to the staff). That flag was used until 1902, when the design from the state seal was added to the blue stripe.

On July 1, 1956, Georgia adopted a distinctive new flag. The banner kept the seal and blue stripe, but the three horizontal stripes were removed and replaced with the Confederate Battle Flag (a red flag with a blue cross of St. Andrew containing 13 stars). People who opposed the new design claimed that the banner recalled slavery and racism. Those who supported the design argued that it was a symbol of their Southern heritage. In the mid-1990's, Governor Zell Miller led an unsuccessful campaign to replace the flag with a new design.

On Jan. 24, 2001, Georgia's House of Representatives adopted a new flag design. The flag was legalized on Jan. 31, 2001. However, the design was not popular and by early 2003, efforts had begun to replace the banner.

A new design was approved by Georgia's legislature and signed into law on May 8, 2003. In March 2004, Georgia residents voted to accept the banner. The new design is similar to the Confederate Stars and Bars. It has three broad stripes—red, white, and red—with a blue canton. The canton features the state coat of arms and the motto *In God We Trust* in yellow, surrounded by a circle of 13 white stars. The stars symbolize Georgia's position as 1 of the 13 original U.S. states.

STATE DATA

Popular name: The Empire State of the South

Capital: Atlanta

Song: "Georgia on My Mind"

Motto: *Wisdom, Justice, and Moderation*

Bird: Brown thrasher

Flower: Cherokee rose

Tree: Live oak

Executive: Governor

Largest cities: Atlanta, Augusta, Columbus, Savannah, Athens, Macon

Land area: 58,930 mi² (152,627 km²), including 1,011 mi² (2,618 km²) of inland water, but excluding 47 mi² (123 km²) of coastal water

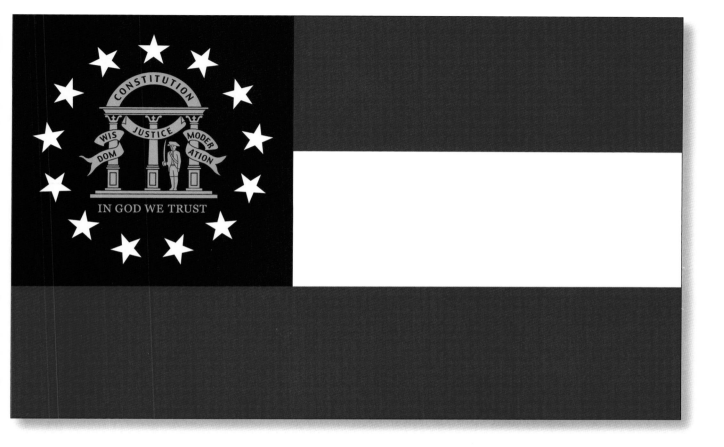

☀ FLAG DATA ☀

- The state flag of Georgia features a field with stripes of equal width—red, white, and red—and a blue canton containing the state coat of arms surrounded by a circle of 13 white stars.

- The most common width-to-length ratios for the flag are 2 to 3, 3 to 5, and 5 to 8.

D2 ABOUT HAWAII

Hawaii is the southernmost state of the United States and is the only state not on the North American mainland. Hawaii lies in the Pacific Ocean about 2,500 miles (4,023 kilometers) southwest of the mainland.

Hawaii consists of 8 large volcanic islands and over 100 small ones. Oahu, the most populous island, consists of two mountain ranges separated by a wide valley. Hawaii, the biggest island, has the state's highest mountains and two active volcanoes.

Polynesian people settled the present-day Hawaiian islands about 2,000 years ago. British Captain James Cook (1728–1799) visited the islands in 1778. European and American missionaries, traders, and farmers followed. A local chief named Kamehameha (1758?–1819) unified the islands and established a monarchy in the early 1800's. Hawaii became a territory of the U.S. in 1898 and gained statehood in 1959.

On Dec. 7, 1941, Japanese warplanes attacked Pearl Harbor on Oahu, propelling the U.S. into World War II (1939–1945). Since the war, tourism and military spending have boosted Hawaii's economy.

Hawaii's population is diverse. In addition to descendants of Polynesian peoples, there are people of European, Japanese, or other Asian ancestry.

ABOUT THE FLAG OF HAWAII

In 1794, British captain George Vancouver presented the Union Jack, the United Kingdom's national flag, to King Kamehameha I of Hawaii. At this time, Kamehameha was uniting the islands into a single kingdom. From 1794 to 1816, the Union Jack flew as the unofficial flag of Hawaii. In 1816, British advisers to the king recommended that he add red, white, and blue stripes to the Union Jack. The result was a distinct national flag for the country of Hawaii. After the British briefly occupied Hawaii in 1843, King Kamehameha III set the number of stripes on the national flag at eight, one for each major island. Hawaii also had other flags, including a naval *ensign* (a national flag flown by a naval ship) and a royal banner.

In January 1893, Americans helped overthrow the Hawaiian government. At that time, the Stars and Stripes was hoisted over the islands. The following year, the new leaders proclaimed Hawaii a republic under its former national flag. On Aug. 12, 1898, however, Hawaii was annexed by the United States. The former national flag of the kingdom and the republic was adopted unchanged. Sixty-one years later, when Hawaii was admitted to the Union as the 50th state, the banner was reconfirmed as the state flag.

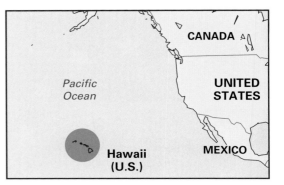

STATE DATA

Popular name: The Aloha State

Capital: Honolulu

Song: "Hawaii Ponoi" ("Hawaii's Own")

Motto: *Ua Mau ke Ea o ka Aina i ka Pono* (The Life of the Land Is Perpetuated in Righteousness)

Bird: Nene (Hawaiian goose)

Flower: Yellow hibiscus

Tree: Kukui

Executive: Governor

Largest urban areas: Honolulu, Hilo, Kailua, Kaneohe, Waipahu, Pearl City

Land area: 6,459 mi^2 (16,729 km^2), including 36 mi^2 (93 km^2) of inland water

☀ FLAG DATA ☀

- The state flag of Hawaii features alternating horizontal stripes of equal width—white, red, and blue—with the Union Jack in the *canton* (the upper corner of a flag, closest to the staff).

- The flag's width-to-length ratio is 1 to 2.

C4 ABOUT IDAHO

Idaho is a Western state of the United States. It takes it name from the Idaho Territory, established in 1863, of which it was a part, along with present-day Montana and Wyoming.

The Rocky Mountains region covers all of Idaho's northern "panhandle." Stretching across the southern part of the state is the Columbia Plateau, which includes the wide, fertile Snake River plain. The plateaus and valleys of the Basin and Range Region occupy southeastern Idaho.

Indians lived in what is now Idaho more than 10,000 years ago. In 1805, explorers Meriwether Lewis (1774–1809) and William Clark (1770–1838) visited the region. Later, fur traders, Mormons from nearby Utah, and gold prospectors arrived. After 1900, irrigation projects attracted farmers.

People of European ancestry make up much of Idaho's population. Today, service industries rank as the state's main employer. Tourism to Idaho's dramatic landscape and recreational facilities is an important industry. Idaho produces more potatoes than any other state, and factories in the state manufacture computer-related products.

ABOUT THE FLAG OF IDAHO

In 1866, the Idaho Territory adopted a seal that showed mountains beneath a new moon, a steamship on the Shoshone River, figures representing Liberty and Peace, and an elk's head. A similar seal was adopted for the new state on March 14, 1891. On the seal, a rising sun replaced the moon, and a miner replaced the figure representing Peace. The 1891 seal currently appears on Idaho's state flag. Created by Emma Edwards Green, it is the only such American design created by a woman.

Idaho's first state flag was adopted by its legislature on March 12, 1907. The flag had a simple blue *field* (background) bearing the name of the state. Later, the state seal was added to the flag by C. A. Elmer, a brigadier general in the National Guard. The addition allowed Idaho's flag to conform to the general pattern of other state flags, which were based on the colors of their Union army regiments. Elmer's design was made legal on March 15, 1927. A standard pattern for the seal was adopted in 1957.

STATE DATA

Popular name: The Gem State

Capital: Boise

Song: "Here We Have Idaho"

Motto: *Esto Perpetua* (Let It Be Perpetual)

Bird: Mountain bluebird

Flower: Syringa

Tree: Western white pine

Executive: Governor

Largest cities: Boise, Nampa, Pocatello, Idaho Falls, Meridian, Coeur d'Alene

Land area: 83,574 mi² (216,456 km²), including 823 mi² (2,131 km²) of inland water

✳ FLAG DATA ✳

- The state flag of Idaho features a dark blue field bearing the name of the state and its official seal.

- The flag's width-to-length ratio is 26 to 33.

C4 ABOUT ILLINOIS

Illinois is a state in the Midwestern region of the United States. The state's name comes from the spelling and pronunciation by French settlers of Iliniwek, the name of the Indians living in the region when the settlers arrived in the late 1600's.

Illinois is largely covered by fertile plains. Parts of the northwest and the south are hilly.

Prehistoric mound-builder Indians left large earthen structures that still stand in what is now Illinois. When French explorers first arrived in the late 1600's, they found many Indian tribes. The area became part of the French colony of Louisiana. In 1763, France lost its North American empire to Great Britain. American settlers took control of the area in the late 1700's.

Many settlers arrived in Illinois between 1820 and 1830. People of European ancestry now make up most of Illinois's population. About 15 percent of the state's people are African Americans.

Agriculture, manufacturing, service industries, and transportation are the principal elements of Illinois's economy. Chicago, the state's chief city, is the transportation center of the United States and the financial capital of the Midwest.

ABOUT THE FLAG OF ILLINOIS

On July 6, 1915, Illinois's legislature adopted a flag that was developed in a contest sponsored by the Daughters of the American Revolution. The flag was a white banner with symbols from the state's seal. These symbols included a rock on a stretch of land with water and the rising sun behind it, along with a shield bearing the national Stars and Stripes in the claws of a bald eagle. A ribbon in the eagle's beak carried the motto of Illinois: *State Sovereignty—National Union*. The dates 1818 (for Illinois statehood) and 1868 (for the first use of the state seal) were shown on the rock.

Some Illinois residents complained that the flag could not be easily identified when flown alongside other state flags. As a result, a law that changed the design went into effect on July 1, 1970. The new design included the sun that appeared on the state seal. The flag's various colors were made standard. And the name of the state was added beneath the seal in blue lettering.

STATE DATA

Popular name: The Land of Lincoln

Capital: Springfield

Song: "Illinois"

Motto: *State Sovereignty, National Union*

Bird: Cardinal

Flower: Native violet

Tree: White oak

Executive: Governor

Largest cities: Chicago, Rockford, Aurora, Naperville, Peoria, Springfield

Land area: 56,343 mi² (145,928 km²), including 750 mi² (1,941 km²) of inland water, but excluding 1,575 mi² (4,079 km²) of Great Lakes water

ILLINOIS

✺ FLAG DATA ✺

- The state flag of Illinois features a white *field* (background) with the state seal in the center. The seal includes a bald eagle, a shield, and a ribbon inscribed with the state motto.

- The width-to-length ratios for the flag are 2 to 3, 3 to 5, 5 to 8, and 10 to 19.

C4 ABOUT INDIANA

Indiana is a state in the Midwestern region of the United States. It was named for the Indiana Territory of which it was a part. The territory was largely inhabited by Indians when the U.S. Congress created it out of the Northwest Territory in 1800.

Northern Indiana is a fertile lowland skirting Lake Michigan. A fertile plain covers the center of the state. Southern Indiana is hilly with lowlands along the Ohio River.

Prehistoric mound-builder Indians lived in what is now Indiana. Few Native Americans remained when the French first explored the area in 1679. Various tribes, driven from their lands to the east, settled in the region during the 1700's and 1800's. The United States made the area part of the Northwest Territory in 1787.

Descendants of German, Irish, and English settlers who arrived in the 1800's and early 1900's today constitute Indiana's largest population groups.

Service industries, manufacturing, and agriculture make up most of Indiana's economy. The state is a leading producer of motor-vehicle parts and pharmaceuticals.

ABOUT THE FLAG OF INDIANA

In 1916, the centennial of Indiana statehood, the Daughters of the American Revolution held a flag design contest. The winning design, by Indiana artist Paul Hadley, was made the official state banner on May 31, 1917. The flag has a blue *field* (background) with a symbol that includes a torch and stars. According to Indiana law, the symbol is either gold or buff (light tan), although gold or golden-yellow is almost always used.

The torch is a symbol of enlightenment and liberty. It has rays that spread outward from its flames. A total of 19 stars ring the torch, recalling that Indiana was the 19th state to join the Union. The name of the state is shown above the largest star. The flag was defined as the "state banner," because a 1901 Indiana law had declared that the state's flag was the Stars and Stripes of the United States. In 1955, Indiana's General Assembly changed the flag's definition from state banner to state flag "in addition to the American flag."

STATE DATA

Popular name: The Hoosier State

Capital: Indianapolis

Song: "On the Banks of the Wabash, Far Away"

Motto: *The Crossroads of America*

Bird: Cardinal

Flower: Peony

Tree: Tulip-poplar (yellow-poplar)

Executive: Governor

Largest cities: Indianapolis, Fort Wayne, Evansville, South Bend, Gary, Hammond

Land area: 36,185 mi^2 (93,720 km^2), including 315 mi^2 (816 km^2) of inland water, but excluding 235 mi^2 (608 km^2) of Great Lakes water

✳ FLAG DATA ✳

- The state flag of Indiana features a dark blue field with a gold or buff (light tan) torch surrounded by 19 stars.

- The flag's width-to-length ratios are 2 to 3 or 3 to 5.

 ABOUT IOWA

Iowa is a state in the Midwestern region of the United States. It takes its name from an Indian tribe that lived in the area. Most of Iowa's land consists of rolling plains that were created by glaciers when they retreated north.

Prehistoric mound-builder Indians left more than 10,000 burial mounds in what is now Iowa. When the first Europeans arrived in the late 1600's, Woodland and Plains Indians lived throughout the area. In 1682, René-Robert Cavelier, Sieur de La Salle (1643–1687), claimed for France the entire region drained by the Mississippi River and named it Louisiana. The claim included Iowa, which became part of the U.S. with the Louisiana Purchase of 1803.

Most Iowans are descendants of Dutch, German, Irish, English, Norwegian, and Swedish settlers. Hispanic Americans, African Americans, and Asian Americans make up small minorities. Agriculture and such related industries as food processing are central to Iowa's economy. The state is the top hog producer in the U.S., and corn is its leading source of farm income. Service industries today employ two-thirds of Iowa's workers.

ABOUT THE FLAG OF IOWA

In the early 1900's, many U.S. states adopted their first official flags. In Iowa, the Daughters of the American Revolution took an active role in creating the state flag. The organization recommended a white banner bearing a flying bald eagle and a ribbon carrying the state motto: *Our Liberties We Prize and Our Rights We Will Maintain.*

The state's name appeared below the ribbon. The War Council of Iowa, set up to coordinate the state's involvement in World War I (1914–1918), approved that flag. Examples of the banner were sent with Iowa troops to Europe. Official adoption of the flag was delayed, however. A Civil War veterans' group, the Grand Army of the Republic, was opposed to any state flag. The veterans felt that they and their dead comrades had fought to preserve the Union. They believed that a state flag went against the ideal of national unity. As a result, the term "state banner" was used to avoid the term "state flag."

On March 29, 1921, the banner was finally approved, with two additions: A blue stripe was added to the *hoist* (the part of the flag closest to the staff) and a red stripe was added to the *fly* (the free end of a flag, farthest from the staff). The design, created by Dixie C. Gebhardt, a member of the Daughters of the American Revolution, recalled the French Tricolor, France's national flag, which flew over Iowa before the Louisiana Purchase of 1803.

STATE DATA	
Popular name: The Hawkeye State	
Capital: Des Moines	
Song: "The Song of Iowa"	
Motto: *Our Liberties We Prize and Our Rights We Will Maintain*	
Bird: Eastern goldfinch (American goldfinch)	
Flower: Wild rose	
Tree: Oak	
Executive: Governor	
Largest cities: Des Moines, Cedar Rapids, Davenport, Sioux City, Waterloo, Iowa City	
Land area: 56,276 mi² (145,754 km²), including 401 mi² (1,038 km²) of inland water	

✳ FLAG DATA ✳

- The state flag of Iowa features two vertical stripes of equal width—blue and red—flanking a wider white stripe. On the white stripe is the state's name below a bald eagle in flight.

- The most common width-to-length ratios for the flag are 2 to 3, 3 to 5, and 5 to 8.

C4 ABOUT KANSAS

Kansas is a state in the center of the United States mainland. This Midwestern state lies on a rolling plain that increases in elevation from east to west.

The earliest inhabitants of what is now Kansas were probably the Kansa, Osage, Pawnee, and Wichita Indian tribes. The first European explorers arrived in 1541. France controlled much of the region from the late 1600's until 1803, when it sold the land to the United States. As a U.S. territory, Kansas became a battleground in the conflict over slavery in the mid-1850's. From the 1860's to the 1880's, Kansas became famous for its cowboys and cattle drives. Depression and drought brought hardships to Kansans in the 1930's.

Most Kansans are of European descent. Less than 1 percent are American Indians. More than half the people live in metropolitan areas, mainly in the eastern half of the state.

The economy of Kansas relies heavily on service industries, but manufacturing and agriculture are also important. Kansas is the nation's leading producer of wheat.

ABOUT THE FLAG OF KANSAS

In Kansas, a distinction was made between the "state banner" and the "state flag." A state banner was first adopted on February 27, 1925. The banner had a blue *field* (background) and the name of the state written above the state seal. The seal was framed by a sunflower, which had been adopted as the state flower in 1903. On June 30, 1953, the state banner was simplified. The name of the state and the seal were removed, leaving a large sunflower blossom on a blue background. The sunflower had a brown center and gold petals. Neither banners were widely used in Kansas.

The Kansas state flag, used to represent the state on official occasions, was adopted on March 23, 1927. It showed the state seal without the inscriptions on its outer rim. Above the seal was the crest of Kansas: a sunflower over a *torse* (a twisted band or wreath) of yellow and blue. In 1961, the state's name was added below the seal in large golden letters. Changes have also been made in the seal's design. In 1985, for example, it was decided that the homesteader's cabin in the seal should no longer have smoke pouring from its chimney. At the same time, the number of bison in the herd was changed to five.

STATE DATA

Popular name: The Sunflower State

Capital: Topeka

Song: "Home on the Range"

Motto: *Ad Astra per Aspera* (To the Stars Through Difficulties)

Bird: Western meadowlark

Flower: Sunflower

Tree: Cottonwood

Executive: Governor

Largest cities: Wichita, Overland Park, Kansas City, Topeka, Olathe, Lawrence

Land area: 82,282 mi^2 (213,110 km^2), including 459 mi^2 (1,189 km^2) of inland water.

KANSAS

☀ FLAG DATA ☀

- The state flag of Kansas features a dark blue field with a sunflower emblem and the state seal above the name of the state in golden-yellow lettering.

- The flag's width-to-length ratio is 3 to 5.

C4 ABOUT KENTUCKY

Kentucky is a state that lies on the border between the North and the South of the United States. The Ohio River forms Kentucky's long northern border. An area of gently rolling pastures called the Bluegrass Region covers north-central Kentucky. A rugged coalfield lies in the northwest. Along the Mississippi River, western Kentucky has wide flood plains with cypress swamps. Farmland stretches along the state's southern border. Eastern Kentucky is mountainous.

The first people lived in what is now Kentucky as long as 12,000 years ago. Early European explorers found many American Indian tribes in the region. Colonial settlement began in the 1770's.

Almost 90 percent of Kentucky's people are of European descent. About 7 percent are of African ancestry.

Service industries, manufacturing, coal mining, and agriculture all contribute to the state's economy. Kentucky is the nation's leading producer of bourbon whiskey and the world's top producer of burley tobacco. The Kentucky Derby, held annually since 1875, is the nation's oldest continually run horse race.

ABOUT THE FLAG OF KENTUCKY

When Kentucky was admitted to the Union in 1792, it was considered to be on the nation's western frontier. Kentucky's former status as a frontier state is reflected in the symbolism of its state seal. The seal's current design, officially adopted on June 14, 1962, shows two men embracing. One of the men is a frontiersman in deerskin clothing. The other is a gentleman in formal coat and pants. The two men represent Kentucky's country and city residents of 1792, as well as Westerners and Easterners with a common interest in preserving national unity. That theme is also reflected in the state motto, *United We Stand, Divided We Fall.*

The Kentucky seal has been displayed in the center of the state flag since the banner was adopted on March 26, 1918. A blue *field* (background) is used in about half of all American state flags. Surrounding the seal is a wreath of goldenrod (the state flower) and the name *Commonwealth of Kentucky*. Like Virginia, Pennsylvania, and Massachusetts, Kentucky has designated itself a commonwealth.

STATE DATA

Popular name:	The Bluegrass State
Capital:	Frankfort
Song:	"My Old Kentucky Home"
Motto:	*United We Stand, Divided We Fall*
Bird:	Kentucky cardinal
Flower:	Goldenrod
Tree:	Tulip-poplar (yellow-poplar)
Executive:	Governor
Largest cities:	Lexington, Louisville, Owensboro, Bowling Green, Covington, Hopkinsville
Land area:	40,411 mi² (104,665 km²), including 679 mi² (1,758 km²) of inland water

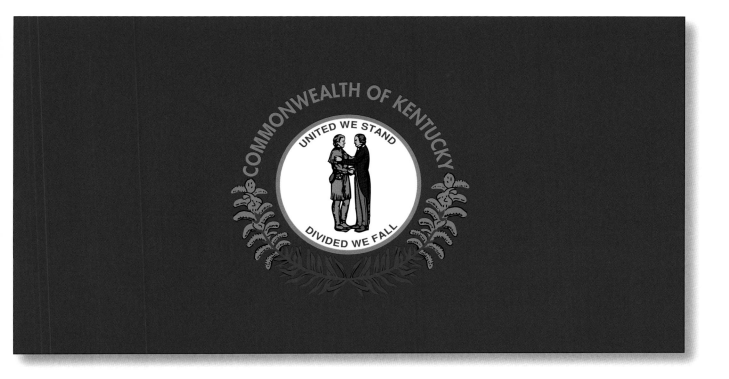

☀ FLAG DATA ☀

- The state flag of Kentucky features a dark blue field with the state seal in the center.

- The flag's width-to-length ratio is 10 to 19.

ABOUT LOUISIANA

Louisiana is a state in the southeastern United States. At the toe of this boot-shaped state, the Mississippi River empties into the Gulf of Mexico. Louisiana lies in a fertile lowland dotted with lakes and bayous.

American Indians from about 30 tribes lived in what is now Louisiana when the first European explorers arrived in the mid-1500's. The region was claimed for France in 1682 and named Louisiana in honor of the French king, Louis XIV (1638–1715). France sold Louisiana to the United States in 1803.

Louisiana's population groups include *Creoles*, descendants of early French and Spanish settlers; *Cajuns*, descendants of later French settlers from Canada; whites of Anglo-Saxon ancestry; and blacks of African or mixed African and European heritage. More than 70 percent of all Louisianans live in urban areas.

A majority of Louisiana's people work in tourism and other service industries, the largest sector of the state's economy. Manufacturing, mineral production, and fishing are other important economic activities. Louisiana is the world's leading producer of crayfish.

ABOUT THE FLAG OF LOUISIANA

During the Civil War (1861–1865), Louisiana adopted a flag that resembled the Stars and Stripes. Louisiana's flag, however, had stripes of red, white, and blue and a red *canton* (the upper corner of a flag, next to the staff) with a single yellow star. This flag incorporated the colors of France and Spain, former colonial rulers of Louisiana, as well as the colors of the United States. In 1912, the 100th anniversary of Louisiana's statehood, the state legislature adopted the current flag design with the pelican in the center.

The pelican was used as a symbol of Louisiana as early as 1812. It appeared on the state seal, as well as on some unofficial flags. The current flag shows a pelican tearing at its breast to feed its young. Real pelicans never do this, but from the Middle Ages (from about the 400's through the 1400's), this symbol has represented self-sacrifice and dedication to the young.

STATE DATA

Popular name: The Pelican State

Capital: Baton Rouge

Songs: "Give Me Louisiana" and "You Are My Sunshine"

Motto: *Union, Justice, and Confidence*

Bird: Brown pelican

Flower: Magnolia

Tree: Baldcypress

Executive: Governor

Largest cities: New Orleans, Baton Rouge, Shreveport, Metairie, Lafayette, Lake Charles

Land area: 47,717 mi² (123,586 km²), including 4,153 mi² (10,757 km²) of inland water, but excluding 1,931 mi² (5,002 km²) of coastal water

✳ FLAG DATA ✳

- The state flag of Louisiana features a blue *field* (background) with a pelican and its young in a nest above a ribbon bearing the state motto, *Union, Justice, and Confidence*.

- The most common width-to-length ratios for the flag are 2 to 3, 3 to 5, and 5 to 8.

C4 ABOUT MAINE

Maine, the largest of the New England States in area, is the easternmost state in the United States. A region of coastal lowlands follows Maine's shoreline along the North Atlantic Ocean. Inland from that region, the terrain rises gradually into the White Mountains. Forests cover nearly 90 percent of the state.

Algonquian Indians lived in what is now Maine when European explorers arrived in the 1500's. English settlement began in the early 1600's. Maine was part of Massachusetts for about 170 years before it became a state in 1820.

Nearly all of Maine's people were born in the United States. Many are of English, French, Irish, French-Canadian, or German ancestry. Most of the people live near the coast in the southwestern part of the state.

Maine's extensive forests provide raw materials for many products. Mills in Maine make lumber, paper, toothpicks, and other wood products. Fishing is also an important industry. Maine's lobster catch is greater than that of any other state. Service industries also contribute greatly to Maine's economy.

ABOUT THE FLAG OF MAINE

Until 1820, Maine was a district of Massachusetts, and its early symbols reflected that connection. The pine tree emblem that had been adopted for the Massachusetts naval flag in April 1776, for example, was featured on Maine's coat of arms when it became a state. Pine trees, used to build ships, were important to the early economy of the region.

A buff (light tan) flag with a pine tree and the North Star was adopted as the state flag on March 21, 1901. The star was a fitting symbol, because Maine was the northernmost U.S. state for many years. The current state flag was adopted in February 1909. Its coat of arms shows an emblem of a moose and a pine tree on a shield. A farmer stands on one side of the shield, while a sailor stands on the other. A ribbon below the shield carries the state name. Above the shield is the North Star and the Latin motto *Dirigo* (I Direct, or I Guide). Maine also has a special naval flag that resembles the naval flag of Massachusetts. It is a white banner with a green pine tree.

STATE DATA

Popular name: The Pine Tree State

Capital: Augusta

Song: "State of Maine Song"

Motto: *Dirigo* (I Direct, or I Guide)

Bird: Chickadee

Flower: White pine cone and tassel

Tree: White pine

Executive: Governor

Largest cities: Portland, Lewiston, Bangor, South Portland, Auburn, Brunswick

Land area: 33,128 mi² (85,801 km²), including 2,263 mi² (5,862 km²) of inland water, but excluding 613 mi² (1,587 km²) of coastal water

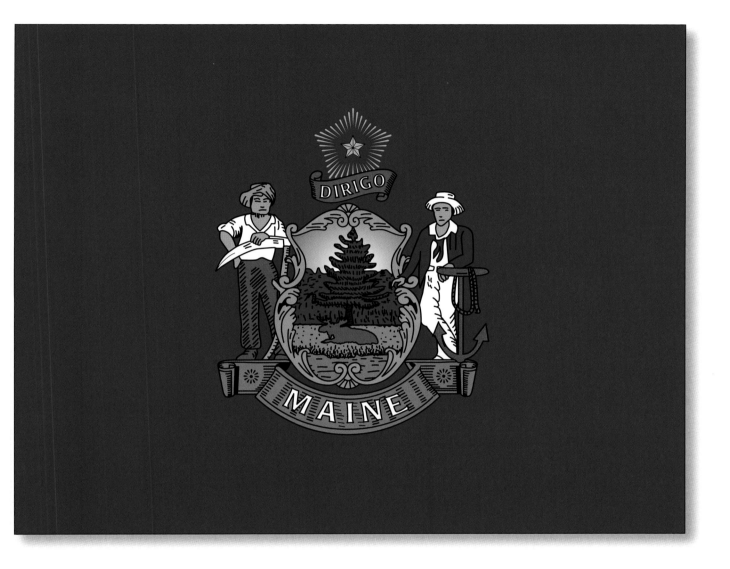

✸ FLAG DATA ✸

- The state flag of Maine features a dark blue *field* (background) with the state coat of arms in the center.

- The flag's width-to-length ratio is 26 to 33.

C4 ABOUT MARYLAND

Maryland is a densely populated state at the northern corner of the Southern States. The Atlantic Coastal Plain covers the eastern part of Maryland on both sides of Chesapeake Bay. A region of low, rolling hills and fertile valleys, called the Piedmont, stretches between the coastal plain and a mountainous region in the west.

American Indians lived in what is now Maryland as early as 10,000 B.C. European explorers arrived in the A.D. 1500's. The English Calvert family controlled the area throughout much of the 1600's and 1700's. Maryland was a key battleground during the War of 1812 and the American Civil War (1861–1865).

Most of Maryland's people live in the densely populated Baltimore metropolitan area or close to Washington, D.C. The state's ethnic groups include people of European, African, American Indian, and Asian descent.

Maryland's economy depends mainly on service industries, especially those related to the federal government. The Baltimore area is a major center for manufacturing and trade.

ABOUT THE FLAG OF MARYLAND

Of the 13 original states, Maryland alone has a state flag based on a banner flown under British rule. During colonial times, the flag used to represent Maryland was the personal banner of the Lords Baltimore, who controlled the colony. In 1638, Leonard Calvert, son of the first Lord Baltimore, wrote to his brother that he had flown the Calvert banner in battle. Through the rest of the 1600's and into the 1700's, the flag continued to be used.

The Calvert coat of arms was made up of six vertical stripes, three yellow and three black. A diagonal stripe of alternating yellow and black ran from the upper *hoist* (the part of the flag closest to the staff) to the lower *fly* (the free end of a flag, farthest from the staff). There is no known symbolism attached to the flag's colors or design. The Crossland family, the family of the first Lord Baltimore's mother, had a coat of arms with clear symbolism. It made a pun on the family's name by showing a white and red shield with a red and white *cross botoné*, or a cross with arms ending in three balls.

During the American Revolution (1775–1783), symbols associated with heraldry were rarely used in the 13 British colonies. However, the arms of Lord Baltimore were never forgotten in Maryland. Various designs used through the years included elements from the Baltimore coat of arms. During the Civil War (1861–1865), for example, Maryland troops wore badges with symbols based on the arms.

On March 9, 1904, a banner combining the arms of the Calverts and the Crosslands was officially adopted as Maryland's state flag. Many flagpoles that fly the state banner have a cross botoné as the *finial* (the ornament at the top of the pole).

STATE DATA

Popular name: The Old Line State

Capital: Annapolis

Song: "Maryland, My Maryland"

Motto: *Fatti Maschii Parole Femine* (Manly Deeds, Womanly Words)

Bird: Baltimore oriole

Flower: Black-eyed Susan

Tree: White oak

Executive: Governor

Largest cities: Baltimore, Columbia, Silver Spring, Dundalk, Wheaton-Glenmont, Ellicott City

Land area: 10,455 mi² (27,077 km²), including 680 mi² (1,761 km²) of inland water, but excluding 1,842 mi² (4,771 km²) of coastal water

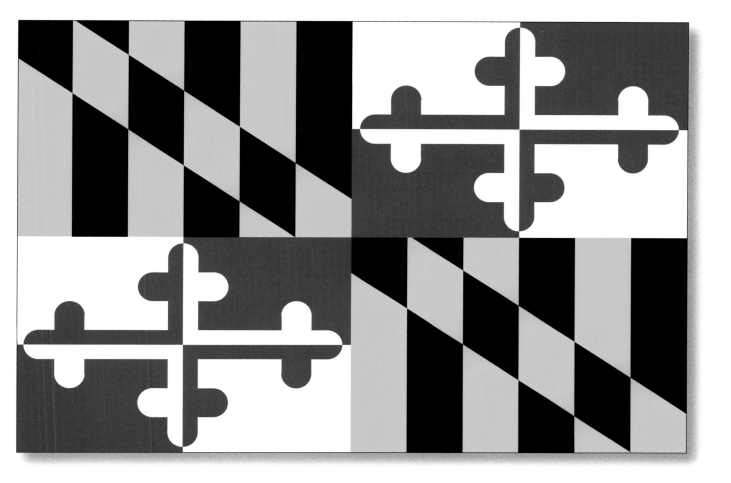

✳ FLAG DATA ✳

- The state flag of Maryland features a quartered design of alternating red-white and black-yellow panels.

- The most common width-to-length ratios for the flag are 2 to 3, 3 to 5, and 5 to 8.

ABOUT MASSACHUSETTS

Massachusetts is a small state in the New England region of the northeastern United States. Massachusetts has alternating low-land and upland regions extending from the North Atlantic Ocean to the Taconic Mountains on the state's far western edge. Forests cover more than half the land.

People lived in what is now Massachusetts more than 10,000 years ago. Early inhabitants included the Massachuset and other Algonquian American Indian tribes. The first Europeans to visit the area were probably the Vikings, who sailed to North America about A.D. 1000. The Pilgrims arrived in 1620 and the Puritans in 1630. Many important American events that happened either right before or during the Revolutionary War (1775–1783) took place in Massachusetts.

Most of the state's people were born in the United States. Population groups include people of Western European, Hispanic, African, and Asian ancestry. More than 90 percent of the people live in urban areas.

The economy of Massachusetts is based on service industries, including tourism, education, banking, and trade. Manufacturing and commercial fishing are other important industries.

ABOUT THE FLAG OF MASSACHUSETTS

In 1629, the seal of the Massachusetts Bay Colony showed an Indian and pine trees. Both of these symbols are still used in Massachusetts. In 1686, a pine tree was added to the cross of St. George (a flag that represents England) to create a special local flag used in other parts of New England. On April 29, 1776, a white flag with a green pine tree and the motto *Appeal to Heaven* was made the Massachusetts naval *ensign* (a national flag flown by a naval ship). A similar flag was flown during the American Revolutionary War by Washington's Cruisers.

In 1780, the Indian figure from the 1629 seal was placed on the coat of arms for the new Commonwealth of Massachusetts. The Indian appears in gold on a blue shield. A silver star, symboliz-ing statehood, is also included. The arm and sword in the crest, together with the Latin motto on the sur-rounding ribbon, refer to lines writ-ten in the 1600's by the English politician Algernon Sidney. The motto is *Ense Petit Placidam sub Libertate Quietem* (By the Sword We Seek Peace, but Peace Only Under Liberty). The coat of arms on a white *field* (background) was used as regimental colors by many Massachusetts troops before 1908.

The first official nonmilitary state flag was adopted by the Massachusetts legislature on March 18, 1908. The front of the flag fea-tured the state's coat of arms. The reverse side featured a green pine tree on a blue shield. In 1971, the pine tree shield was removed, and the coat of arms was placed on both sides of the state banner. However, Massachusetts still uses the pine tree on a plain white flag as its naval banner.

STATE DATA

Popular name: The Bay State

Capital: Boston

Song: "All Hail to Massachusetts"

Motto: *Ense Petit Placidam sub Libertate Quietem* (By the Sword We Seek Peace, But Peace Only Under Liberty)

Bird: Black-capped chickadee

Flower: Mayflower

Tree: American elm

Executive: Governor

Largest cities: Boston, Worcester, Springfield, Lowell, Cambridge, Brockton

Land area: 8,262 mi^2 (21,398 km^2), including 424 mi^2 (1,098 km^2) of inland water, but excluding 979 mi^2 (2,536 km^2) of coastal water

✷ FLAG DATA ✷

- The state flag of Massachusetts features a white field with a coat of arms showing an American Indian and a star.

- The flag's width-to-length ratio is 1 to 1⅗, but ratios of 2 to 3, 3 to 5, and 4⅓ to 5½ are also acceptable.

C4 ABOUT MICHIGAN

Michigan, a state in the Midwestern United States, is made up of two peninsulas. These two separate land areas are connected by the Mackinac Bridge. The Lower Peninsula is a plains region. Farther north, the smaller Upper Peninsula is rugged and hilly. The state borders all the Great Lakes except Lake Ontario. Michigan has the longest shoreline of any state but Alaska.

American Indians lived in what is now Michigan when French explorers arrived in the early 1600's. French and British fur traders later struggled for control of the area. In 1787, as part of the Northwest Territory, the region came under United States control.

Almost all of Michigan's people were born in the United States. Most are of European descent. About 14 percent are African Americans. Most of the state's people live in metropolitan areas in the southern half of the Lower Peninsula. Only about 3 percent of the people live in the Upper Peninsula.

Michigan is the nation's top manufacturer of automobiles and is second only to Minnesota in iron ore production. Michigan also is an important farming and tourist state.

ABOUT THE FLAG OF MICHIGAN

Michigan's coat of arms, based on its state seal, has three Latin mottoes: *E Pluribus Unum* (One Out of Many); *Tuebor* (I Will Defend); and *Si Quæris Peninsulam Amoenam, Circumspice* (If You Seek a Pleasant Peninsula, Look About You). The central design of the shield shows a man with a rifle standing on a peninsula and the sun setting over water. The coat of arms is supported on either side by an elk and a moose. The elk and moose may have been based on the coat of arms of the Hudson's Bay Company, a fur trading company that became active in the region in the 1600's. A bald eagle serves as the crest, or decoration, at the top of a shield. The coat of arms was adopted in 1835. It has been used ever since, with only a few minor changes.

In 1837, a Michigan military company called the Brady Guard was given its colors by the state's first governor, Stevens T. Mason. Mason was known as the "Boy Governor" because he was elected when he was just 23 years old. The flag of the Brady Guard was a silk banner with the new state seal on the *obverse* (the side of a coin, medal, flag, or the like, that features the principal design) of the flag. This type of design was popular with U.S. military units at the time. Michigan formally adopted blue military colors in 1865. In 1911, it adopted a state flag of the same color.

STATE DATA

Popular name: The Wolverine State

Capital: Lansing

Song: "Michigan, My Michigan" (unofficial)

Motto: *Si Quæris Peninsulam Amoenam, Circumspice* (If You Seek a Pleasant Peninsula, Look About You)

Bird: Robin

Flower: Apple blossom

Tree: White pine

Executive: Governor

Largest cities: Detroit, Grand Rapids, Warren, Flint, Sterling Heights, Lansing

Land area: 58,513 mi^2 (151,548 km^2), including 1,704 mi^2 (4,412 km^2) of inland water, but excluding 38,192 mi^2 (98,917 km^2) of Great Lakes water

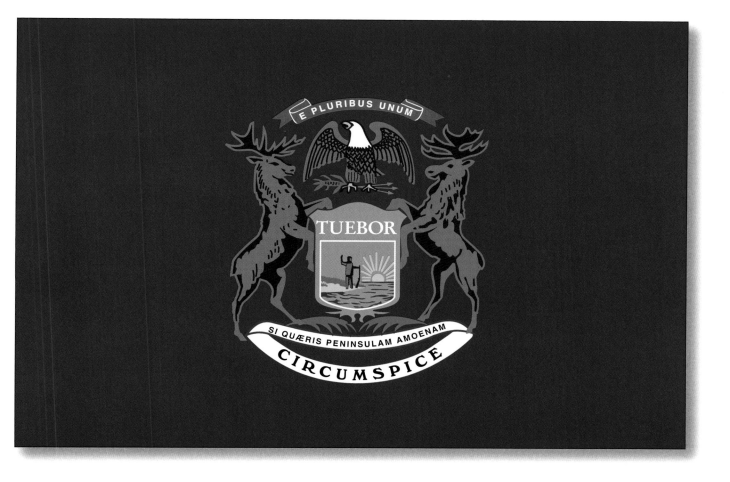

✳ FLAG DATA ✳

- The state flag of Michigan features a dark blue *field* (background) with the state coat of arms in the center.

- The most common width-to-length ratios for the flag are 2 to 3, 3 to 5, and 5 to 8.

ABOUT MINNESOTA

Minnesota is a large state in the Midwestern United States. Most of the state lies on gently rolling plains, more than half of which are farmland and about a third forested. Minnesota has thousands of lakes.

Sioux Indians lived in what is now Minnesota when European explorers and fur traders arrived in the late 1600's. The United States acquired the land from the British and French in the late 1700's and early 1800's. The area attracted many lumberjacks, farmers, and miners.

Most Minnesotans are of European ancestry. African Americans, Asians, and Hispanics each make up about 3 percent of the state's population. More than half of Minnesota's people live in the Minneapolis-St. Paul metropolitan area. Nearly 20 percent live in other urban areas.

Minnesota's economy depends chiefly on such service industries as banking, tourism, and trade. Health care is another important industry in the state; the Mayo Clinic in Rochester is a world-famous medical center. Manufacturing and agriculture also provide important income.

ABOUT THE FLAG OF MINNESOTA

Minnesota's first state flag, designed by Mrs. Edward H. Center of Minneapolis, was adopted in 1893. The *obverse* (the side of a coin, medal, flag, or the like, that features the principal design) of the flag was white with the state seal, the name of the state, and 19 gold stars symbolizing Minnesota as the 19th state to follow the original 13 states into the Union. The *reverse* (back) side of the flag was plain blue. This flag was not widely used, in part because the design was not easy to manufacture in quantity.

On March 19, 1957, a new design was adopted. The flag's *field* (background) was blue on both sides. The central design of the 1893 flag was placed on a white disk and displayed on both sides of the banner.

On August 1, 1983, changes were made to the state seal. Previously, the American Indian in the seal had been shown riding away from a rural area where a farmer plowed the earth. The farmer's musket and powder horn rested nearby. The revised design still includes the Indian and other symbols. However, the new shield avoids the original suggestion that development requires the land's original inhabitants to leave the area. Other symbols that were retained in the seal include an image of St. Anthony Falls, a setting sun, and a border of lady's-slipper flowers. The dates of the first European settlement in Minnesota (1819), its admission to the Union (1858), and the adoption of the first state flag (1893) were also retained. The state motto, *L'Etoile du Nord* (The Star of the North), is shown on a red ribbon.

STATE DATA

Popular name: The Gopher State

Capital: St. Paul

Song: "Hail! Minnesota"

Motto: *L' Etoile du Nord* (The Star of the North)

Bird: Common loon

Flower: Pink and white lady's-slipper

Tree: Norway pine

Executive: Governor

Largest cities: Minneapolis, St. Paul, Duluth, Rochester, Bloomington, Brooklyn Park

Land area: 84,397 mi^2 (218,587 km^2), including 4,780 mi^2 (12,381 km^2) of inland water, but excluding 2,546 mi^2 (6,594 km^2) of Great Lakes water

✸ FLAG DATA ✸

- The state flag of Minnesota features a blue field with the state seal in the center.

- The most common width-to-length ratios for the flag are 2 to 3, 3 to 5, and 5 to 8.

ABOUT MISSISSIPPI

Mississippi is a state in the southeastern United States. The Mississippi River forms most of the state's western border. The fertile alluvial plain that extends along the western edge of the state is known to most Mississippians as the Delta. Except for a long, narrow prairie in the northeast, the rest of Mississippi lies on a coastal plain mostly covered with low, rolling, forested hills.

The first inhabitants of Mississippi were American Indians. The region was ruled by the powerful Chickasaw, Choctaw, and Natchez tribes when the first European explorers arrived in the mid-1500's. French colonists brought the first black slaves to the region from Africa in the 1700's.

Mississippi today has a larger proportion of African Americans than any other state—36 percent. Just over 1 percent of Mississippians are Hispanic Americans. The rest of Mississippi's people are mainly of European or American Indian ancestry. The entire population is almost evenly divided between urban and rural areas.

Mississippi's economy depends heavily on service industries, including casino gaming and telecommunications. Mississippi is a leading producer of upholstered furniture, cotton, and chickens.

ABOUT THE FLAG OF MISSISSIPPI

A section of what is today the state of Mississippi was part of the West Florida Republic. The republic was formed in 1810 by American settlers in the area who were opposed to Spanish rule. Its flag had a blue *field* (background) with a single white star in the center. It was flown again on Jan. 9, 1861, when Mississippi seceded from the United States. The blue and white banner became known throughout the South as the Bonnie Blue Flag. On Jan. 26, 1861, Mississippi adopted the Magnolia Flag, a banner with a white field and a magnolia tree in its center. The Bonnie Blue Flag appeared in the *canton* (the upper corner of a flag, next to the staff) of the Magnolia Flag. The Magnolia Flag was rarely used after the end of the Civil War (1861–1865). However, the magnolia was designated Mississippi's official state tree in 1938.

In 1894, a new state flag was adopted by Mississippi's legislature. It is still in use today. The banner has three horizontal stripes of blue, white, and red, similar to the Stars and Bars of the Confederate States of America. The Confederate Battle Flag appears in the banner's canton. In 1996, a white *fimbriation* (a narrow border separating two colors) was made standard to separate the canton from the blue and red stripes.

People in Mississippi were deeply divided over the 1894 design. Opponents of the design said that it recalled slavery and racist traditions. Supporters argued that the design represented state pride and Southern heritage. In 2000, Mississippi's Supreme Court determined that the state flag had not been mentioned in the revised state's statutes in 1906. As a result, the flag had ceased to be legal at that time. On April 17, 2001, Mississippi voters chose to retain the 1894 design instead of adopting a new design that omitted the Confederate Battle Flag.

STATE DATA

Popular name: The Magnolia State

Capital: Jackson

Song: "Go Mis-sis-sip-pi"

Motto: *Virtute et Armis* (By Valor and Arms)

Bird: Mockingbird

Flower: Magnolia

Tree: Magnolia

Executive: Governor

Largest cities: Jackson, Gulfport, Biloxi, Hattiesburg, Greenville, Meridian

Land area: 47,695 mi² (123,530 km²), including 781 mi² (2,024 km²) of inland water, but excluding 591 mi² (1,530 km²) of coastal water

✳ FLAG DATA ✳

- The state flag of Mississippi features three horizontal stripes of equal width—blue, white, and red—with the Confederate Battle Flag in the canton.

- The flag's width-to-length ratio is 2 to 3.

C4 ABOUT MISSOURI

Missouri is a state in the Midwest region of the United States. The Missouri River winds across the state from west to east. Fertile, rolling land once covered by glaciers lies north of the river. The hilly Ozark region, one of the nation's major tourist areas, takes up most of the land south of the river and features forests, caves, lakes, springs, and streams.

The earliest known inhabitants of what is now Missouri were American Indians who built large earthwork mounds, many of which still exist. Various Indian tribes lived in the region when French explorers arrived. France claimed the region in 1682 and sold it to the United States in 1803.

Most of Missouri's people are of European descent. About 11 percent of the people are African Americans. Another large population group is made up of American Indians. About two-thirds of Missourians live in urban areas.

Service industries provide the largest share of Missouri's economy. Such industries include tourism, health care, professional sports franchises, trade, and banking. Missouri is a leading producer of transportation equipment and processed food and beverages. Agriculture is also important to the state's economy.

ABOUT THE FLAG OF MISSOURI

Missouri's state seal, which incorporates the state coat of arms, was adopted on Jan. 11, 1822. The coat of arms is circled by a belt with the inscription *United We Stand, Divided We Fall*. It is divided down the middle, with the coat of arms of the United States on the right half and a crescent and bear on the left half. In *heraldry*, the crescent is a traditional symbol that stands for a second son. (Heraldry is the study of the symbols and designs used on coats of arms, flags, seals, and badges.) On the state seal, the crescent refers to the fact that Missouri was the second state to be created out of the Louisiana Territory. The crescent also symbolizes the growing wealth and population of the state. The bear is a grizzly bear, once native to the area. Two similar bears stand on either side of the shield. The Latin motto beneath them reads *Salus Populi Suprema Lex Esto* (The Welfare of the People Shall Be the Supreme Law). In the *crest*, or top decoration of the coat of arms, are 23 stars with one larger star rising to join them. The large star represents Missouri's status as the 24th state to join the Union. The 24 stars are repeated on a blue ring that surrounds the central design. Also within the coat of arms are a helmet (representing self-government) and the Roman numerals for 1820 (the year the U.S. Senate passed the Missouri Compromise).

The flag's background has three horizontal stripes of red, white, and blue, referring both to the United States and to the short-lived Confederate States of America. Both governments recognized a separate Missouri state government during the Civil War (1861-1865). The state flag was created in 1909 and was adopted on March 22, 1913. The designer, Marie Elizabeth Watkins Oliver, was a member of the Daughters of the American Revolution, the group responsible for the creation of a number of other state flags.

STATE DATA

Popular name: The Show Me State

Capital: Jefferson City

Song: "Missouri Waltz"

Motto: *Salus Populi Suprema Lex Esto* (The Welfare of the People Shall Be the Supreme Law)

Bird: Bluebird

Flower: White hawthorn blossom

Tree: Flowering dogwood

Executive: Governor

Largest cities: Kansas City, St. Louis, Springfield, Independence, Columbia, St. Joseph

Land area: 69,709 mi² (180,546 km²), including 811 mi² (2,100 km²) of inland water

☀ FLAG DATA ☀

- The state flag of Missouri features three horizontal stripes of equal width—red, white, and blue—with a central coat of arms.

- The flag's width-to-length ratio is 7 to 12.

C4 ABOUT MONTANA

Montana is a large state in the northwestern United States. The Rocky Mountains in the western part of the state take up about 40 percent of Montana's land. The Great Plains stretch eastward to cover the rest.

The first inhabitants of what is now Montana were American Indians from many tribes. French trappers may have visited the area as early as the 1740's. The United States acquired eastern Montana from France in 1803, and the rest of the state from the United Kingdom in 1846.

Most of Montana's people are of European ancestry. About 6 percent are American Indians, most of whom live on reservations. Slightly more than half the people live in urban areas. Montana is one of the least populated states.

Montana's economy is based on service industries, including tourism, health care, trade, government, and real estate. Mining and agriculture are also important. Montana is the nation's top producer of talc, and eastern Montana has the nation's largest coal reserves. Some of the largest U.S. cattle ranches are in Montana.

ABOUT THE FLAG OF MONTANA

In 1865, Montana's provisional, or temporary, legislature adopted a seal for public business. That same design continues to be used by the state today. It includes an image of the Rocky Mountains, which are an important part of the state's geography. The state's name is derived from the Spanish word *montana*, which means "mountainous." A river and forests on the seal recall Montana's natural beauty and its wealth in forestry and farming. The seal also includes an image of Great Falls, a Montana landmark that has become a tourist attraction. The plow and crossed pick and shovel symbolize agriculture and the mining industry. The state's motto, *Oro y Plata* (Gold and Silver), also refers to the mining industry. The motto is displayed on a ribbon in the seal.

The state flag was based on the flag of the First Montana infantry regiment in the Spanish-American War (1898). The original design was dark blue with the state seal in the center. Montana law stated that the official state flag should have fringe on its top and bottom edges only. The flag was adopted in 1905. However, many other states adopted similar designs, and the flag became hard to distinguish from other state banners. As a result, the word *Montana* was added above the seal in 1981.

STATE DATA

Popular name: The Treasure State

Capital: Helena

Song: "Montana"

Motto: *Oro y Plata* (Gold and Silver)

Bird: Western meadowlark

Flower: Bitter root

Tree: Ponderosa pine

Executive: Governor

Largest cities: Billings, Missoula, Great Falls, Butte, Bozeman, Helena

Land area: 147,047 mi² (380,849 km²), including 1,409 mi² (3,859 km²) of inland water

✳ FLAG DATA ✳

- The state flag of Montana features a dark blue *field* (background) with the name of the state in yellow above the state seal.

- The flag's width-to-length ratios are 3 to 5 for home use and 5 to 8 when officially displayed in a public location.

C4 ABOUT NEBRASKA

Nebraska is a large state in the central United States. Plains cover the entire state. The land is rolling and fertile in the east but hilly and sandy in the central and western parts of the state.

Prehistoric people probably lived in what is now Nebraska as long as 25,000 years ago. The earliest modern-day inhabitants of the region were American Indians. European explorers first reached the area in the A.D. 1500's. The United States bought the land from France in 1803. American pioneers settled in Nebraska throughout the 1800's.

Most Nebraskans are of European descent. About 4 percent of the population are of Mexican ancestry. More than half the state's people are concentrated in urban areas, mostly in the east.

Farms cover 95 percent of Nebraska, a larger percentage than any other state. Nebraska is a leading producer of beef cattle, hogs, corn, and soybeans, and its factories produce food products, chemicals, and machinery. However, the largest share of the state's economy comes from service industries, including health care and trade.

Government services are another important service industry in Nebraska, which is the only state with a unicameral (one-house) state legislature.

ABOUT THE FLAG OF NEBRASKA

In 1925, Nebraska adopted a state flag. Many people had been in favor of a state flag for Nebraska, including Mrs. B. Miller, who wrote "The Flag Song of Nebraska." The flag's design features the state seal, which was created by Nebraska politician Isaac Wiles and approved in 1867, the year Nebraska became a state. Nebraska's seal colors are gold and silver.

Nebraska's seal shows the Missouri River with a steamboat, a smith with a hammer and anvil, a settler's cabin, wheat sheaves and stalks of corn, and a train of cars heading toward the Rocky Mountains (which lie west of Nebraska). The motto *Equality Before the Law* refers to the right of each Nebraska settler to public land. Some historians have suggested that the motto may also refer to the struggle for civil rights that was being carried on when the seal was adopted in 1867.

Nebraska's legislature designated the flag a state banner in 1925. In 1963, the banner's status was raised to that of official state flag.

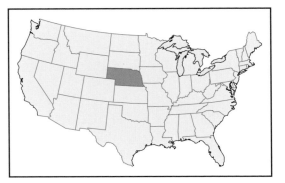

STATE DATA

Popular name: The Cornhusker State

Capital: Lincoln

Song: "Beautiful Nebraska"

Motto: *Equality Before the Law*

Bird: Western meadowlark

Flower: Goldenrod

Tree: Cottonwood

Executive: Governor

Largest cities: Omaha, Lincoln, Bellevue, Grand Island, Kearney, Fremont

Land area: 77,359 mi^2 (200,358 km^2), including 481 mi^2 (1,245 km^2) of inland water

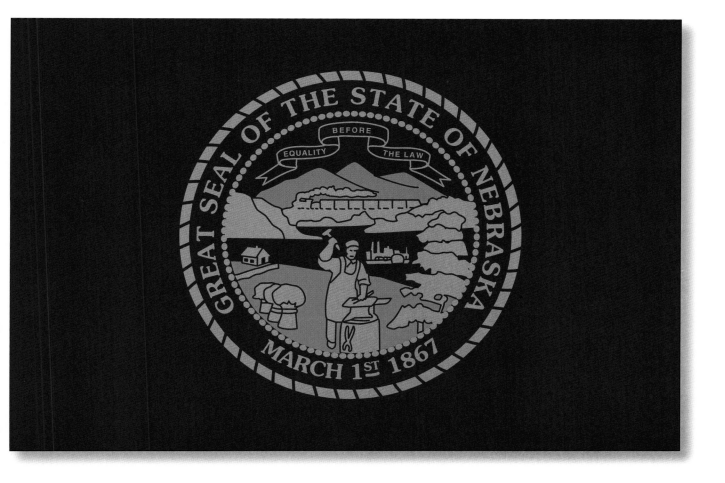

✳ FLAG DATA ✳

- The state flag of Nebraska features a dark blue *field* (background) with the state seal in the center.

- The most common width-to-length ratios for the flag are 2 to 3, 3 to 5, and 5 to 8.

C4 ABOUT NEVADA

Nevada, a large state in the western United States, receives less rainfall than any other state. Although Nevada has snow-capped mountains and grassy valleys, a huge desert area, called the Great Basin, covers almost the entire state.

American Indians have lived in what is now Nevada for thousands of years. European fur traders and trappers began to explore the area in the early A.D. 1800's. The United States acquired the land from Mexico in 1848. Today, the federal government owns about 80 percent of Nevada's land, the largest percentage of any state.

A majority of Nevada's people are of European ancestry. About 20 percent are Hispanic and about 7 percent African American. Nearly all of the state's people live in the metropolitan areas surrounding Las Vegas and Reno, Nevada's two largest cities. Nevada has about a dozen Indian reservations.

Nevada is the nation's leader in both gold and silver mining, but the state's economy depends mainly on tourism. Ski resorts, hotels, and casinos attract many visitors to the state. Nevada also is the only state that legally allows most forms of gambling statewide.

ABOUT THE FLAG OF NEVADA

An early Nevada state flag, used from 1905 to 1915, had silver and gold stars, along with the words *silver*, *Nevada*, and *gold* displayed on a dark blue *field* (background). It was designed by Governor John Sparks and Colonel Harry Day to honor the state's mining industry. The next state flag featured a modified version of the state seal. It included a railroad on a trestle, a wagon

drawn by four horses, a mine, a sheaf of wheat, farming tools, and the sun rising over the mountains. The design was completed by the name of the state, the motto *All for Our Country*, 18 gold stars, and 18 silver stars. The total number of stars referred to Nevada's status as the 36th state to join the Union, which it did in 1864. Many people thought the design of this flag was too elaborate.

In 1926, a new flag design was created by Louis Shellback. At the *hoist* (the part of the flag closest to the staff), the banner featured a half wreath of sagebrush, the state flower, surrounding a silver star and the words *Battle Born*. The words honored Nevada's admission to the Union during the Civil War (1861–1865). The letters of the name of the state were arranged around the star. In 1991, the flag was revised to show the letters of Nevada's name in a single line beneath the star.

STATE DATA

Popular name: The Silver State

Capital: Carson City

Song: "Home Means Nevada"

Motto: *All for Our Country*

Bird: Mountain bluebird

Flower: Sagebrush

Trees: Bristlecone pine and singleleaf piñon

Executive: Governor

Largest cities: Las Vegas, Paradise, Reno, Henderson, Sunrise Manor, Spring Valley

Land area: 110,567 mi² (286,367 km²), including 761 mi² (1,971 km²) of inland water

☀ FLAG DATA ☀

- The state flag of Nevada features a dark blue field with an emblem in the upper hoist corner. The emblem includes a wreath, a star, the name of the state, and the inscription *Battle Born*.

- The most common width-to-length ratios for the flag are 2 to 3, 3 to 5, and 5 to 8.

C4 ABOUT NEW HAMPSHIRE

New Hampshire is a state in the New England region of the northeastern United States. New Hampshire has a small coastline on the Atlantic Ocean. Coastal lowlands give way to an upland region of hills and valleys that extends to the state's western border at the Connecticut River. The rugged White Mountains rise in the north.

Algonquian Indians lived in what is now New Hampshire before European explorers arrived in the early 1600's. English settlement began in the 1620's. On Jan. 5, 1776, New Hampshire became the first of the 13 original American colonies to break away from Great Britain and adopt its own constitution.

Nearly all of New Hampshire's people are of European or Canadian ancestry. About 60 percent of the state's people live in urban areas.

Real estate, banking, insurance, and trade are among the service industries that provide the greatest share of New Hampshire's income. The state's natural beauty and year-round outdoor activities attract many tourists. New Hampshire also is famous for its large granite quarries.

ABOUT THE FLAG OF NEW HAMPSHIRE

The state's first seal was used in 1775. A new seal was created in 1784 after the Revolutionary War (1775–1783). On Dec. 28, 1792, the legislature required regiments in the state militia to carry the national flag and regimental colors displaying the state seal. More than a century passed, however, before a state flag was adopted for general purposes. In 1909, a state flag with a blue *field* (background) and the state seal in the center was officially adopted. The seal was framed by a wreath of laurel leaves interspersed with nine stars. The stars referred to New Hampshire's status as the ninth U.S. state to *ratify* (approve) the U.S. Constitution.

The seal features the frigate *Raleigh*, which was built at Portsmouth. A frigate is a medium-sized sailing warship with three masts. Although the ship was built in 1776, the seal shows it flying the U.S. flag that was adopted in 1777. The seal was slightly altered in 1931.

STATE DATA

Popular name: The Granite State

Capital: Concord

Song: "Old New Hampshire"

Motto: *Live Free or Die*

Bird: Purple finch

Flower: Purple lilac

Tree: White birch

Executive: Governor

Largest cities: Manchester, Nashua, Concord, Derry, Rochester, Salem

Land area: 9,283 mi² (24,044 km²), including 314 mi² (813 km²) of inland water

✹ FLAG DATA ✹

- The state flag of New Hampshire features a dark blue field with the state seal in the center.

- The most common width-to-length ratios for the flag are 2 to 3, 3 to 5, and 5 to 8.

ABOUT NEW JERSEY

New Jersey, which borders the Atlantic Ocean in the eastern United States, is the nation's most densely populated state. All of New Jersey's people live in metropolitan areas.

A gently rolling lowland plain stretches inland from the Atlantic coast to cover the southern 60 percent of New Jersey. An industrial belt called the Piedmont lies north of the coastal plain. Beyond the Piedmont, rocky highlands extend to a mountainous region along the state's northwestern border.

American Indians lived in what is now New Jersey before European settlers arrived in the early 1600's. During the late 1700's, New Jersey was a major battleground in the Revolutionary War (1775–1783).

More than half of New Jersey's people are of European descent. About 14 percent are African Americans, 13 percent Hispanics, and 6 percent Asians.

Although it is a leading industrial state, such service industries as insurance, real estate, tourism, and trade account for the greatest share of New Jersey's economy. The state's manufactured products include pharmaceuticals and processed foods. Agriculture also accounts for an important part of New Jersey's economy.

ABOUT THE FLAG OF NEW JERSEY

New Jersey's state flag was adopted on March 26, 1896. In 1938, a law was passed that clearly stated that the right to fly the flag was not limited to New Jersey's governor alone. The flag is the only one of the 50 state flags to have a *field* (background) of buff, or light tan. The buff color is based on the facings, or trim, of the uniforms worn by New Jersey troops during the Revolutionary War in America. The 13 original states, including New Jersey, all had their colors assigned by George Washington, commander in chief of the Continental Army, on Oct. 2, 1779.

New Jersey's coat of arms appears in the center of its state flag. It is also found in the state seal. The coat of arms was designed by the artist Eugène du Simitière. The seal was adopted by the state legislature on Oct. 3, 1776. The three plows on the arms stand for farming, which is also represented by the goddess Ceres, who stands with her cornucopia to one side of the shield. On the other side of the shield is Liberty, displaying a liberty cap. The horse's head on the *crest* (the decoration at the top of a coat of arms) was shown on early New Jersey coins.

STATE DATA

Popular name: The Garden State

Capital: Trenton

Motto: *Liberty and Prosperity*

Bird: Eastern goldfinch

Flower: Violet

Tree: Red oak

Executive: Governor

Largest cities: Newark, Jersey City, Paterson, Elizabeth, Edison, Woodbridge

Land area: 7,790 mi² (20,175 km²), including 371 mi² (960 km²) of inland water, but excluding 425 mi² (1,102 km²) of coastal water

✻ FLAG DATA ✻

- The state flag of New Jersey features a field of buff with the state coat of arms in the center.

- The most common width-to-length ratios for the flag are 2 to 3, 3 to 5, and 5 to 8.

C4 ABOUT NEW MEXICO

New Mexico is a large state in the southwestern United States. The Great Plains cover the eastern third of the state. The southwestern third includes rugged mountains and broad desert basins. Northwestern New Mexico features sharp cliffs, deep canyons, and flat-topped hills called *mesas*. The Rocky Mountains rise in north-central New Mexico.

American Indians have lived in what is now New Mexico for at least 10,000 years. Spanish explorers reached the area in the early A.D. 1500's. After many years of rule, first by Spain and then Mexico, the region became a U.S. possession in 1848.

New Mexico has higher percentages of American Indians and Hispanics than any other state. Indians make up nearly 10 percent of the population and Hispanics about 42 percent. Most of the rest of the state's people are of European descent. Most New Mexicans live in urban areas. Many of the state's people speak both English and Spanish.

New Mexico's economy depends heavily on service industries, especially tourism. Mining and agriculture are also important sources of state revenue.

ABOUT THE FLAG OF NEW MEXICO

The original state flag of New Mexico was designed by historian Ralph E. Twitchell and adopted in 1915. The flag had a blue *field* (background) with the name of the state, the number 47, the state seal, and a U.S. flag. (The number 47 represented New Mexico's status as the 47th U.S. state.)

Unlike other American state flags, the current flag of New Mexico is very simple in design. Its colors are based on the colors of Queen Isabella of Castile that were brought to the New World by the Spanish Conquistadors. The present flag was designed by the archaeologist and physician Harry Mera. Mera's design was chosen in a competition sponsored by the Daughters of the American Revolution. The banner was officially adopted in March 1925. Shown on the flag is the Zia sun symbol, an ancient symbol of the Zia Pueblo people. The shape of this symbol influenced the design of the capitol building in Santa Fe.

STATE DATA

Popular name: The Land of Enchantment

Capital: Santa Fe

Song: "O, Fair New Mexico"

Motto: *Crescit Eundo* (It Grows as It Goes)

Bird: Roadrunner

Flower: Yucca flower

Tree: Piñon, or nut pine

Executive: Governor

Largest cities: Albuquerque, Las Cruces, Santa Fe, Rio Rancho, Roswell, South Valley

Land area: 121,599 mi² (314,939 km²), including 234 mi² (605 km²) of inland water

☀ FLAG DATA ☀

- The state flag of New Mexico features a yellow field with a red Zia Indian sun symbol in the center.

- The flag's width-to-length ratio is 2 to 3.

C4 ABOUT NEW YORK

New York is a large state in the Middle Atlantic region of the United States. The state's varied landscape includes a coastal plain, fertile lowlands, hilly uplands, a rocky plateau, and rugged mountains. New York City, in the southeast corner of the state, is the nation's largest city.

Algonquian and Iroquois Indian groups lived in what is now New York before European settlers arrived in the early 1600's. From the late 1600's to the late 1700's, New York was a major battleground in the French and Indian Wars (fought between 1689–1763) and the Revolutionary War in America (1775–1783).

New York has an ethnically diverse population. About 20 percent of New York's population was born in another country. A majority of the population is of European descent. About 16 percent are African Americans and about 5 percent Puerto Ricans.

New York has a varied economy. Service industries provide the largest share of the state's income, but New York is also a leading manufacturing state and one of the nation's top dairy-farming regions.

ABOUT THE FLAG OF NEW YORK

New York's coat of arms features a sun, two *supporters* (figures that stand on either side of a shield or emblem), and the motto *Excelsior* (Ever Upward) on a ribbon. Beneath the sun is a scene showing a view of the Hudson River. One shield supporter is Liberty, shown with her *liberty cap* on a staff. (A liberty cap is a soft, cone-shaped hat with no brim. Such caps were given to slaves in Ancient Rome when they were freed and, because of that, the cap became a symbol of liberty.) The other supporter shown is Justice. A bald eagle perches on a globe on the top of the shield.

In the 1600's, Scandinavian immigrant Jonas Bronck settled on land in what is today the Bronx, a section of New York City. Bronck's coat of arms showed a rising sun. This emblem may have influenced the state seal of New York and its coat of arms, adopted in 1778. However, the sun may have been chosen to honor the Duke of York, who ruled the English colony after 1664. The sun appeared on the badge of the dukes of York.

A banner resembling the current state flag was carried by a military unit during the Revolutionary War. In 1858, a similar flag with a *field* (background) of white was recognized as New York's state flag. The color buff (light tan) replaced the white field on April 8, 1896. (During the Revolutionary War, New York military uniforms used buff-colored facings, or trim.) Five years later, however, the field was changed to dark blue. The coat of arms, although made standard by an 1882 law, is basically the same design that was first adopted during the Revolutionary War.

STATE DATA

Popular name: The Empire State

Capital: Albany

Song: "I Love New York"

Motto: *Excelsior* (Ever Upward)

Bird: Bluebird

Flower: Rose

Tree: Sugar maple

Executive: Governor

Largest cities: New York City, Buffalo, Rochester, Yonkers, Syracuse, Albany

Land area: 49,112 mi² (127,200 km²), including 1,888 mi² (4,891 km²) of inland water, but excluding 4,877 mi² (12,632 km²) of Great Lakes and coastal water

✳ FLAG DATA ✳

- The state flag of New York features a dark blue field with a central coat of arms.

- The flag's width-to-length ratio is 10 to 19.

ABOUT NORTH CAROLINA

North Carolina is a state in the southern United States with a coastline on the Atlantic Ocean. Islands, reefs, and sand bars line North Carolina's long coast. Swamps and farmland lie west of the coast. Much of the western part of the state is mountainous.

More than 30,000 Indians, belonging to some 30 tribes, lived in the region of North Carolina before the Europeans arrived. North Carolina's Roanoke Island became the site of the first English settlements in what is now the United States in 1585 and 1587. During the Revolutionary War in America (1775–1783), North Carolina was the first colony to instruct its delegates at the Continental Congress to vote for independence. The state fought on the side of the Confederacy (the Southern States) during the Civil War (1861–1865).

North Carolina's population groups include people of English, German, Irish, and Scottish ancestry. African Americans make up about 22 percent of North Carolina's population.

Service industries make up two-thirds of North Carolina's economy, but manufacturing is the single most important economic activity in the state. The leading manufactured goods are chemicals and tobacco products. North Carolina is the top producer of tobacco products in the United States. It also leads the nation in the production of textiles and household furniture.

ABOUT THE FLAG OF NORTH CAROLINA

During the Revolutionary War in America, a flag was used in North Carolina that had a white *field* (background) with a hornet's nest and the date May 20, 1775. On that day, the town of Mecklenburg, North Carolina, is said to have proclaimed its independence from Britain.

North Carolina's first official flag, adopted on June 22, 1861, was based on the Confederate Stars and Bars. The banner also included the date of North Carolina's secession from the Union, May 20, 1861. It is said that various Confederate regiments used this flag during the Civil War.

The present North Carolina flag, adopted on March 9, 1885, is similar to the state's Civil War banner. One of the flag's ribbons carries the date May 20, 1775. In place of the date of secession, however, the other date shown is April 12, 1776. On that date North Carolina authorized its delegates to the Continental Congress to vote for independence.

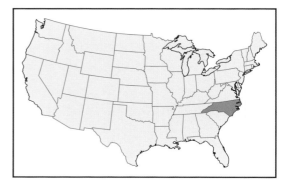

STATE DATA

Popular name: The Tar Heel State

Capital: Raleigh

Song: "The Old North State"

Motto: *Esse Quam Videri* (To Be, Rather Than to Seem)

Bird: Cardinal

Flower: Dogwood

Tree: Pine

Executive: Governor

Largest cities: Charlotte, Raleigh, Greensboro, Durham, Winston-Salem, Fayetteville

Land area: 52,672 mi² (136,421 km²), including 3,954 mi² (10,241 km²) of inland water

✸ FLAG DATA ✸

- The state flag of North Carolina features two horizontal stripes of equal width—red and white—with a vertical blue stripe at the *hoist* (the part of the flag closest to the staff). The blue stripe carries a white star, the initials of the state *(NC)*, and two ribbons with dates inscribed.

- The flag's width-to-length ratio is 3 to 4.

C4 ABOUT NORTH DAKOTA

North Dakota is a Midwestern state that lies in the center of the North American continent. North Dakota's landscape generally rises from east to west. The flat Red River Valley in the east of the state has some of the world's most fertile farmland. Rolling plains cover the center of the state. The Badlands, in North Dakota's southwest, is a region of wind- and water-carved formations of sandstone, shale, and clay.

Six groups of Indians, including the Sioux, lived in North Dakota when Europeans arrived. Most of what is now North Dakota was gained by the United States as part of the Louisiana Purchase in 1803. In the early 1870's, the arrival of the Northern Pacific Railroad and the availability of free land brought increasing numbers of settlers.

About 44 percent of North Dakotans live in rural areas. People of German and Norwegian descent make up the state's largest population groups.

Service industries make up the largest portion of North Dakota's economy. Farming, however, is more important to North Dakota than most states, and wheat is the chief crop. North Dakota leads the states in the production of flaxseed, sunflower seeds, and barley. The state also has huge deposits of lignite coal and large oil reserves.

ABOUT THE FLAG OF NORTH DAKOTA

In the late 1800's, a military unit in the territory of North Dakota flew a blue flag with a coat of arms similar to the U.S. coat of arms in the center. After North Dakota joined the Union in 1889, a similar design was used by the state's National Guard. In 1898–1899, Dakota troops commanded by Major (later Colonel) John H. Fraine fought under the flag in the Philippines. After he returned to North Dakota, Fraine led a drive to have the banner recognized as the state flag. The drive was successful, and the flag was adopted as of March 3, 1911.

In the mid-1900's, a new coat of arms was created. The coat of arms was placed on a flag with a green *field* (background). The flag was adopted by North Dakota's governor and the National Guard on March 15, 1957. The governor's flag also includes four stars, one in each corner. However, the flag did not replace the 1911 banner.

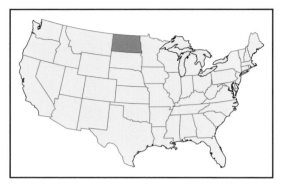

STATE DATA

Popular name: The Flickertail State

Capital: Bismarck

Song: "North Dakota Hymn"

Motto: *Liberty and Union, Now and Forever, One and Inseparable*

Bird: Western meadowlark

Flower: Wild prairie rose

Tree: American elm

Executive: Governor

Largest cities: Fargo, Bismarck, Grand Forks, Minot, Mandan, Dickinson

Land area: 70,704 mi² (183,123 km²), including 1,710 mi² (4,428 km²) of inland water

✳ FLAG DATA ✳

- The state flag of North Dakota features a dark blue field with a coat of arms in the center. The arms include an eagle with outspread wings above a scroll with the words *North Dakota.*

- The flag's width-to-length ratio is 26 to 33.

ABOUT OHIO

Ohio is a Midwestern state in the United States. Lake Erie forms much of Ohio's northern border, and a flat, fertile plain borders the lake. Gently rolling plains with some hills cover western Ohio. A high plateau with steep hills and valleys covers the eastern half of the state.

Ancient Indians called mound builders had highly developed civilizations thousands of years ago in what is now Ohio. Several Indian tribes lived in Ohio when Europeans arrived. The French explorer René-Robert Cavelier, Sieur de La Salle (1643–1687), was probably the first European to reach present-day Ohio, in about 1670. Ohio became part of the Northwest Territory in 1787. Large numbers of settlers began to arrive in the 1790's, after peace treaties were signed with local Indians.

People of German, Irish, or English descent make up Ohio's largest population groups. African Americans make up about 11 percent of the population.

Ohio is an important manufacturing center in the United States. Ohio is among the leading states in the manufacture of chemicals, industrial machinery, motor vehicles and motor vehicle parts, and processed foods. Ohio is also a major producer of corn and soybeans.

ABOUT THE FLAG OF OHIO

Ohio is the only one of the 50 states to use a nonrectangular flag. Created by architect John Eisenmann, the flag's design may have been inspired by the shape of a flag carried by the U.S. cavalry, which was swallow-tailed (forked at the *fly*, the free end of a flag, farthest from the staff). Eisenmann's banner was flown from the Ohio building at the Pan-American Exposition of 1901, a huge fair held in Buffalo, New York. Eisenmann patented his design in 1901 and it became the official state flag on May 9, 1902.

The white circle around the red disk at the *hoist* (the part of the flag closest to the staff) suggests the seed of the buckeye, Ohio's official state tree, as well as the initial letter of the state's name. The stars and stripes and the colors red, white, and blue honor the U.S. national flag. Eisenmann said that the triangles on his design symbolized the state's waterways and roads. The 17 stars on the flag refer to Ohio's status as the 17th state to join the Union. The flag's shape is sometimes called a *burgee*, which is a nautical term for a swallow-tailed flag.

STATE DATA

Popular name: The Buckeye State

Capital: Columbus

Song: "Beautiful Ohio"

Motto: *With God, All Things Are Possible*

Bird: Cardinal

Flower: Scarlet carnation

Tree: Buckeye

Executive: Governor

Largest cities: Columbus, Cleveland, Cincinnati, Toledo, Akron, Dayton

Land area: 41,328 mi^2 (107,040 km^2), including 376 mi^2 (973 km^2) of inland water, but excluding 3,499 mi^2 (9,063 km^2) of Great Lakes water

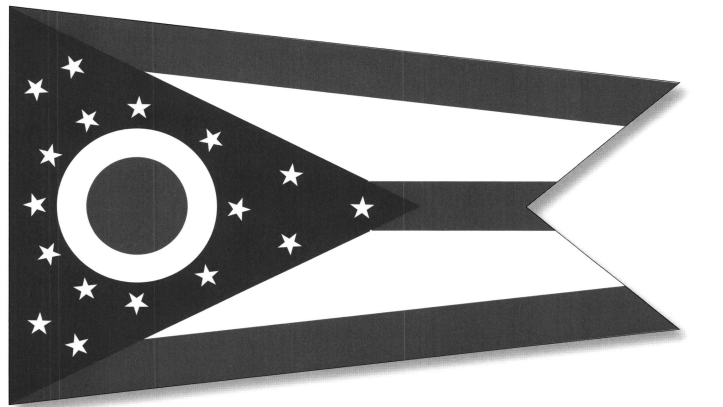

✳ FLAG DATA ✳

- The state flag of Ohio is swallow-tailed and features five horizontal red and white stripes. A blue triangle at the hoist carries a white-bordered red disk and 17 stars.

- The flag's width-to-length ratio is 8 to 13.

ABOUT OKLAHOMA

Oklahoma is a state in the southwestern United States. The northeastern part of Oklahoma is a hilly region with swift streams and steep-sided river valleys. Plains extend across the center and northwestern section of the state. The southeastern and southwestern parts of the state are mountainous.

In the early 1800's, what is now Oklahoma was largely unoccupied. The U.S. government made most of the region into a huge Indian reservation, which became known as Indian Territory. Between 1830 and 1842, the government forced Indians from their homelands in the Southeastern states to Indian Territory. During the late 1880's, the government opened the territory to white settlement. Great land rushes, in which thousands of settlers raced to claim land sites, transformed the region. Whites soon far outnumbered Indians.

Today, American Indians make up about 8 percent of Oklahoma's population. Other population groups in the state include people of German, Irish, or English descent.

Service industries make up the largest part of Oklahoma's economy. The state is a leading producer of natural gas and petroleum. It is also an important producer of wheat and beef cattle.

ABOUT THE FLAG OF OKLAHOMA

Oklahoma adopted its first state flag in 1911. The banner had a red *field* (background) with a central white and blue star. The number 46 was displayed in the star's center. The banner's red field referred to the state's Native American population. The number 46 symbolized Oklahoma's status as the 46th U.S. state. After World War I (1914–1918), some citizens opposed the state flag because it resembled Communist banners.

A new state flag was adopted on April 2, 1925. The flag was created by artist Louise Funk Fluke, based on suggestions from Joseph Thoburn of the Oklahoma Historical Society. The banner features a blue field with the traditional rawhide shield of the Osage Indians. The banner's blue field symbolizes loyalty and devotion. The shield represents the defense of the state. The shield includes small crosses, which commonly stand for stars in Native American art. The olive branch and the *calumet* (Native American peace pipe) were included as emblems of peace between the settlers and Native Americans.

On May 9, 1941, the name of the state was added to the flag's field.

STATE DATA

Popular name: The Sooner State

Capital: Oklahoma City

Song: "Oklahoma!"

Motto: *Labor Omnia Vincit* (Labor Conquers All Things)

Bird: Scissor-tailed flycatcher

Flower: Mistletoe

Tree: Redbud

Executive: Governor

Largest cities: Oklahoma City, Tulsa, Norman, Lawton, Broken Arrow, Edmond

Land area: 69,903 mi² (181,048 km²), including 1,224 mi² (3,171 km²) of inland water

OKLAHOMA

☀ FLAG DATA ☀

- The state flag of Oklahoma features a blue field with a rawhide shield, an olive branch, and a calumet above the name of the state in white lettering.

- The most common width-to-length ratios for the flag are 2 to 3, 3 to 5, and 5 to 8.

C4 ABOUT OREGON

Oregon is a Pacific Coast state of the United States. It is known for its spectacular scenery, which includes vast forests of evergreen trees, the snow-covered peaks of the Cascade Range, a cliff-lined seacoast, and the mighty Columbia River.

Many Indian tribes lived in the region of present-day Oregon before the arrival of Europeans. Fur traders set up posts in what is now Oregon in the early 1800's. In 1834, the first permanent American settlement in the region was set up by Methodist missionaries in the Willamette Valley. The first large group of settlers arrived in Oregon in 1843. The population increased steadily from then on, especially after the completion of the transcontinental railroad.

Some of Oregon's people are descended from pioneers who followed the Oregon Trail. Oregon's largest population groups include people with German, English, Irish, American Indian, Norwegian, French, Italian, Swedish, and Scottish ancestry.

Service industries make up about two-thirds of Oregon's economy. Oregon ranks among the leading states in lumber production. Wheat is Oregon's most valuable food crop. Millions of tourists come to Oregon every year to enjoy the state's natural beauty.

ABOUT THE FLAG OF OREGON

A number of U.S. state flags originally had different designs on the *obverse* (the side of a coin, medal, flag, or the like that features the principal design) and *reverse* (back side). However, because of the expense and difficulty of manufacturing these banners, they were gradually replaced by simpler banners. Oregon is now the only U.S. state with a separate design on the reverse side of its flag. (Paraguay is the only nation to have such a flag.)

The Oregon state flag became official on Feb. 26, 1925. The front of the banner includes the name of the state and the date of its admission to the Union (1859). It also features elements from the state seal, including the Pacific Ocean with ships, mountains, and symbols of mining and farming. A pioneer's covered wagon and the words *The Union* are also displayed on the flag's obverse side. The 33 stars around the outside of the shield refer to Oregon's status as the 33rd U.S. state. The beaver illustration on the reverse side of the flag acknowledges the state's natural resources.

STATE DATA

Popular name: The Beaver State

Capital: Salem

Song: "Oregon, My Oregon"

Motto: *She Flies with Her Own Wings*

Bird: Western meadowlark

Flower: Oregon grape

Tree: Douglas-fir

Executive: Governor

Largest cities: Portland, Eugene, Salem, Gresham, Beaverton, Hillsboro

Land area: 97,052 mi^2 (251,365 km^2), including 1,050 mi^2 (2,718 km^2) of inland water, but excluding 80 mi^2 (207 km^2) of coastal water

❋ FLAG DATA ❋

- The state flag of Oregon features a dark blue *field* (background) with the phrase *State of Oregon*, the date 1859, and an emblem in golden-yellow on the obverse side. A golden-yellow beaver appears on the reverse side of Oregon's flag (not shown).

- The flag's width-to-length ratio is 500 to 833.

ABOUT PENNSYLVANIA

Pennsylvania is a Middle Atlantic state of the United States. Most of the state is made up of hills, plateaus, ridges, and valleys.

Indians lived in the region of present-day Pennsylvania for thousands of years before Europeans arrived. The first Europeans to form a permanent settlement in the region were Swedish. Pennsylvania was a British colony from 1664 until the Revolutionary War in America (1775–1783). The Declaration of Independence was signed in Pennsylvania's State House (now Independence Hall), in Philadelphia, on July 4, 1776. The Constitutional Convention of 1787 was held in Philadelphia. The city was the U.S. capital from 1790 to 1800.

Pennsylvania's largest population groups include people of German, Irish, Italian, English, and Polish descent. About 10 percent of Pennsylvania's people are African Americans.

Although service industries employ four-fifths of Pennsylvania's workers, Pennsylvania is also an important manufacturing state. Chemicals, electrical equipment, and processed foods are Pennsylvania's chief manufactured products. The world's largest chocolate and cocoa factory is located in Hershey. Pennsylvania is also a leading state in coal production.

ABOUT THE FLAG OF PENNSYLVANIA

In 1776 or 1777, a seal was designed for Pennsylvania that was similar to the coat of arms that now appears on the state flag. In 1779, Pennsylvania's legislature approved the use of a coat of arms on the state flag. Different versions of this flag design were used throughout the 1800's. On June 13, 1907, a law was passed describing the state flag. That flag is still used today.

Agriculture and commerce are represented in the coat of arms by the ship and the sheaves of wheat. Some historians think that these symbols may have been derived from the seal of Philadelphia. The plow on the arms may have been borrowed from an earlier coat of arms of Chester County. Pennsylvania's emblem also includes horses in harness, a stalk of corn, and an olive branch. The state motto, *Virtue, Liberty, and Independence*, is displayed on the ribbon below the arms. The *standard* (flag) of the Pennsylvania governor employs the same design on a *field* (background) of white instead of blue.

STATE DATA

Popular name: The Keystone State

Capital: Harrisburg

Song: "Pennsylvania"

Motto: *Virtue, Liberty, and Independence*

Bird: Ruffed grouse

Flower: Mountain laurel

Tree: Hemlock

Executive: Governor

Largest cities: Philadelphia, Pittsburgh, Allentown, Erie, Upper Darby, Reading

Land area: 45,310 mi^2 (117,351 km^2), including 490 mi^2 (1,269 km^2) of inland water, but excluding 749 mi^2 (1,939 km^2) of Great Lakes water

✸ FLAG DATA ✸

- The state flag of Pennsylvania features a dark blue field and a central coat of arms with black horses as *supporters* (figures that stand on either side of a shield).

- The flag's width-to-length ratio is 27 to 37.

C4 ABOUT RHODE ISLAND

Rhode Island, a New England state, is the smallest U.S. state in area. The state is almost cut in half by Narragansett Bay, which extends 28 miles (45 kilometers) inland. The state includes 36 islands. Lowlands with sandy beaches and plains cover much of the state. The northwestern third of Rhode Island has sloping hills and a higher elevation.

Archaeological evidence suggests that Native Americans arrived in the region that includes Rhode Island some 10,000 years ago. Algonquian-speaking tribes were living in the area when European settlers began arriving in the 1630's. A Puritan minister named Roger Williams (1603?–1683) founded a settlement at Providence in 1636 as a place of safety for people fleeing religious persecution. During the Revolutionary War in America (1775–1783), Rhode Islanders helped organize the Continental Navy. Several important advances in industrial technology were achieved by Rhode Islanders, including the first water-powered cotton spinning machines and the invention of methods of gold and silver plating.

Most Rhode Islanders were born in the United States. Of those not born in the U.S., many are of Portugese ancestry.

Service industries account for a large portion of Rhode Island's economy. Rhode Island is a top jewelry-producing state. Recreational activities on Narragansett Bay attract hundreds of thousands of tourists.

ABOUT THE FLAG OF RHODE ISLAND

In 1647, Rhode Island's General Assembly adopted an anchor for its colonial seal. In 1664, the word *Hope* was added to the seal. During the Revolutionary War in America, those symbols were used on military flags.

Rhode Island's first nonmilitary state flag was adopted on March 30, 1877. The banner's white *field* (background) was borrowed from the facings, or trim, on state militia uniforms worn during the Revolutionary War. The flag's anchor and motto were shown in an elaborate style and encircled by 38 blue stars representing the number of states in the Union. On Feb. 1, 1882, that flag was replaced by a simpler design. The new banner had a blue field with a yellow anchor surrounded by a ring of 13 yellow stars. The 13 stars referred to the original Thirteen Colonies, which included Rhode Island.

On May 19, 1897, the current state flag was adopted. The flag features a white field, elements in yellow and blue, similar to those of the state seal, and 13 yellow stars. These colors go against the customs of *heraldry*—the study of the symbols and designs used on coats of arms, flags, seals, and other emblems—because yellow on white is very difficult to see, especially when the flag is flying or seen in poor light.

STATE DATA

Popular name: The Ocean State

Capital: Providence

Song: "Rhode Island's It for Me"

Motto: *Hope*

Bird: Rhode Island Red

Flower: Violet

Tree: Red maple

Executive: Governor

Largest cities: Providence, Warwick, Cranston, Pawtucket, East Providence, Woonsocket

Land area: 1,213 mi^2 (3,142 km^2), including 168 mi^2 (436 km^2) of inland water, but excluding 18 mi^2 (47 km^2) of coastal water

✹ FLAG DATA ✹

- The state flag of Rhode Island features a white field with the state coat of arms surrounded by 13 yellow stars in the center. The arms consist of a yellow anchor and a blue ribbon with the motto *Hope*.

- The flag's width-to-length ratio is 29 to 33.

C4 ABOUT SOUTH CAROLINA

South Carolina is a small Southern state of the United States. The eastern part of South Carolina, known as *Low Country*, is a lowland along the Atlantic Ocean. The area known as *Up Country*, in the west, rises from sand hills to mountains.

Before white settlers arrived in the region, more than 30 Indian tribes lived in what is now South Carolina. The first permanent settlement formed in 1670. South Carolina was the site of many significant battles of the Revolutionary War in America (1775–1783). The Civil War (1861–1865) began in South Carolina. On Dec. 20, 1860, South Carolina became the first state to *secede* (withdraw) from the Union. Then, on April 12, 1861, Confederate troops fired the first shot of the war in an attack on Fort Sumter, in Charleston Harbor.

African Americans make up about 30 percent of South Carolina's population. Other large population groups include people with German, Irish, English, Scotch-Irish, and American Indian ancestry.

South Carolina is one of the leading textile-manufacturing and tobacco-growing states. Beaches, gardens, plantations, historic sites, and charming cities attract many tourists to South Carolina.

ABOUT THE FLAG OF SOUTH CAROLINA

In 1776, a blue flag with a white crescent in its upper *hoist* (the part of the flag closest to the staff) was raised by anti-British forces at a fort in Charleston Harbor. The flag design was based on the blue uniforms and white crescent badges on the caps of the fort's patriot guards, commanded by Colonel William Moultrie. The fort, later renamed Fort Moultrie, was built of palmetto logs. The spongy wood of the logs absorbed the shock of the British cannonballs. As a result, the palmetto was adopted by South Carolinians as their chief state symbol and as an element in new flag designs. In the early 1800's, different "Palmetto Flags" flew over South Carolina.

After South Carolina seceded from the Union in 1860, numerous flag designs were proposed for the state flag. In 1861, South Carolina's legislature adopted a blue flag with a white crescent in the hoist and a white oval and golden palmetto in the center. Two days later, the palmetto was changed to white and the oval was removed. That flag has represented the state ever since.

STATE DATA

Popular name: The Palmetto State

Capital: Columbia

Song: "Carolina"

Mottoes: *Animis Opibusque Parati* (Prepared In Mind and Resources); *Dum Spiro Spero* (While I Breathe, I Hope)

Bird: Carolina wren

Flower: Yellow jessamine

Tree: Palmetto

Executive: Governor

Largest cities: Columbia, Charleston, North Charleston, Greenville, Rock Hill, Mount Pleasant

Land area: 31,117 mi² (80,593 km²), including 1,006 mi² (2,605 km²) of inland water, but excluding 72 mi² (186 km²) of coastal water

✻ FLAG DATA ✻

- The state flag of South Carolina features a dark blue *field* (background) with a white palmetto tree in the center and a white crescent in the upper hoist.

- The most common width-to-length ratios for the flag are 2 to 3, 3 to 5, and 5 to 8.

C4 ABOUT SOUTH DAKOTA

South Dakota is a Midwestern state of the United States. The landscape of eastern South Dakota features low hills, glacial lakes, and fertile cropland. Deep canyons, *buttes* (steep, flat-topped hills), and rolling plains, as well as the famous Black Hills and Badlands, characterize the west.

Two major Indian tribes, the Arikora and the Cheyenne, lived in the South Dakota area before the arrival of European explorers in the mid-1700's. The area that is now South Dakota was part of the historic Louisiana Purchase in 1803. Farmers began to settle in the region in the late 1850's. The discovery of gold brought a rush of settlers and aggravated conflicts with the Indians who lived there. A huge land rush began in 1878, and between 1870 and 1890 the population grew almost 30-fold.

Eight percent of South Dakota's population is American Indian, a higher percentage than in any other state except Alaska or New Mexico. Other large population groups in South Dakota include people of German, Norwegian, Irish, and English ancestry.

About 90 percent of South Dakota is farmland. The chief farm products are beef cattle, corn, soybeans, and wheat. The Black Hills, which include Mount Rushmore National Memorial, attract millions of tourists every year.

ABOUT THE FLAG OF SOUTH DAKOTA

In the early 1900's, Doane Robinson, secretary of the state historical society, worked with state Senator Ernest May to create a flag for South Dakota. The design was first painted by Robinson's secretary, Ida Anding. The banner, influenced by a song written by Willis Johnson, had a sky-blue *field* (background) and a yellow sun with rays. The sun was framed by the name of the state and its nickname, *The Sunshine State*. After South Dakota's legislature added the state seal on the reverse side, the new flag became official on July 1, 1909. However, the expense and difficulty of making a double-sided flag eventually convinced state authorities to combine the banner's two emblems on one side.

On March 11, 1963, the legislature approved a new design for use on both sides of the flag. The design included the same inscriptions and the state seal encircled by golden rays. Another change was made to the flag in 1992, when the state's new nickname—*The Mount Rushmore State*—was substituted for the old nickname. The seal includes the name of the state, the date of its admission to the Union (1889), and the state motto, *Under God the People Rule*. A farmer plowing his fields is shown in the foreground of the seal. The background shows cattle, crops, a furnace for smelting metals, and a steamship on a river.

STATE DATA

Popular name: The Mount Rushmore State

Capital: Pierre

Song: "Hail, South Dakota"

Motto: *Under God the People Rule*

Bird: Ring-necked pheasant

Flower: American pasqueflower

Tree: Black Hills spruce

Executive: Governor

Largest cities: Sioux Falls, Rapid City, Aberdeen, Watertown, Brookings, Mitchell

Land area: 77,122 mi² (199,744 km²), including 1,225 mi² (3,174 km²) of inland water

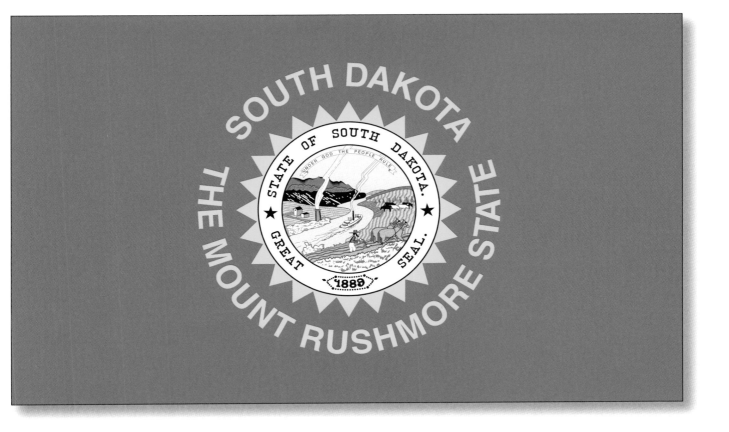

❋ FLAG DATA ❋

- The state flag of South Dakota features a blue field with the state seal in the center, circled by the name of the state and the inscription *The Mount Rushmore State*.

- The flag's width-to-length ratio is 3 to 5.

C4 ABOUT TENNESSEE

Tennessee is a Southern state of the United States. Several mountain ranges, including the Blue Ridge and the Appalachian Ridge, rise in the eastern region of the state. The land slopes downward toward the west to the Mississippi River, which forms Tennessee's western border.

Indians probably lived in what is now Tennessee some 10,000 years ago. At the time white pioneers first settled in the region, in the late 1760's, Tennessee was part of the British colony of North Carolina. However, the Tennessee region was isolated geographically from the main colony, so in 1772 citizens of Tennessee formed their own government and drew up one of North America's first written constitutions. A few years later, Daniel Boone (1734–1820) blazed the Wilderness Road, opening the region to settlement.

About 16 percent of Tennessee's people are African Americans. Tennessee's other large population groups have Irish, German, English, or Scotch-Irish ancestry.

Service industries make up the largest portion of the state's economy, but Tennessee is an important agricultural and mining state. Beef cattle bring in most of Tennessee's farm income, and tobacco is its chief field crop. Processed foods and beverages, transportation equipment, and chemicals top the list of the state's manufactured products. Two of the largest U.S. whiskey distilleries operate in Tennessee. Nashville, Tennessee, is the center of American country and western music.

ABOUT THE FLAG OF TENNESSEE

Tennessee's first official flag was adopted in 1897. The banner had diagonal stripes of red, blue, and white. The state's nickname, *The Volunteer State*, was shown in yellow and the number 16 was shown in blue. The 16 referred to Tennessee's status as the 16th state in the Union.

The current design, created by Captain LeRoy Reeves of the Tennessee Infantry, was approved on April 17, 1905. The *field* (background) of the flag is red with a vertical blue stripe at the *fly* end (the free end of a flag, farthest from the staff). In the center is a blue circle with three white stars. Reeves said that the stars referred to the "three grand divisions of the state," which is interpreted as meaning East, Middle, and West Tennessee. However, the three stars have also been said to represent either the three presidents who lived in Tennessee (Andrew Jackson, James Polk, and Andrew Johnson) or Tennessee's joining the Union as the third state after the original 13. Tennessee and neighboring Arkansas are the only states to have red fields for their flags.

STATE DATA

Popular name: The Volunteer State

Capital: Nashville

Songs: "Rocky Top" and "Tennessee Waltz"

Motto: *Agriculture and Commerce*

Bird: Mockingbird

Flower: Iris

Tree: Tulip-poplar (yellow-poplar)

Executive: Governor

Largest cities: Memphis, Nashville, Knoxville, Chattanooga, Clarksville, Murfreesboro

Land area: 42,146 mi² (109,158 km²), including 926 mi² (2,400 km²) of inland water

✸ FLAG DATA ✸

- The state flag of Tennessee features a red field with a white-bordered blue disk in the center. Three white stars are shown on the disk. At the fly are two unequal vertical stripes of white and blue.

- The flag's width-to-length ratio is 3 to 5.

ABOUT TEXAS

Texas is a Southwestern state of the United States. It has a larger area than any other state except Alaska. Texas's varied landscape ranges from fertile lowlands along the Gulf Coast to rugged and rolling hills, treeless plains, and high mountains.

About 30,000 Indians lived in what is now Texas before the first Europeans arrived. Spanish explorers arrived in the region in the early 1500's. Texas eventually became a colony of Spain. In 1821, Mexico gained its independence from Spain, and Texas became part of Mexico. Americans began to settle in Texas in the 1820's. In 1836, after a war with Mexico that included a famous battle at a Spanish mission called the Alamo, Texas became an independent republic. It joined the United States in 1845.

About 32 percent of Texas's people are of Hispanic origin and about 12 percent are African Americans. Other large ethnic groups include people of German, Irish, and English descent.

Texas has one of the country's largest economies; this economy is largely comprised of service industries. Texas has more farmland than any other state. It also leads all other states in the production of cotton, cattle, sheep, and wool. Texas ranks first among the states in the production and refining of oil and natural gas.

ABOUT THE FLAG OF TEXAS

Before Texas declared its independence from Mexico in 1836, the *Lone Star State* had a number of flags. English-speaking settlers and *filibusters* (people who led revolts against governments of other states

or territories) from the United States flew different banners as symbols of their self-declared "republics." The revolutionary flag established by James Long in 1819 had 13 red and white horizontal stripes and a white star in a red *canton* (the upper corner of a flag, next to the staff). The Fredonia Rebellion flag of 1826 was a banner with two horizontal stripes, white over red.

A number of other striped flags later were used in what is now Texas. One, created by settler Sarah Dodson, had three vertical stripes of blue, white, and red with a star on the stripe at the *hoist* (the part of the flag closest to the staff). That banner is supposed to have been flown on March 2, 1836, the day Texas's independence from Mexico was declared.

The first official Texas flag, used when the region was still part of Mexico, was based on the green, white, and red vertical tricolor of Mexico. It was established on Nov. 3, 1835, for use by local ships. The date 1824 on the center stripe referred to the 1824 Mexican Constitution. That flag is believed to be one of the flags that may have flown at the Alamo when it was attacked by Mexican forces in 1836.

The first official national flag of the Republic of Texas was adopted on Dec. 10, 1836. The banner was blue with a central yellow star. The republic's naval flag was similar to James Long's 1819 banner, except that the canton was blue instead of red. The colors and stripes and star symbols in the naval flag were similar to the U.S. flag. The present state flag was adopted on Jan. 25, 1839. There was no change in the design when Texas became a U.S. state in 1845 or when it joined the Confederacy in 1861.

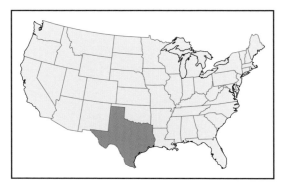

STATE DATA

Popular name: The Lone Star State

Capital: Austin

Song: "Texas, Our Texas"

Motto: *Friendship*

Bird: Mockingbird

Flower: Bluebonnet

Tree: Pecan

Executive: Governor

Largest cities: Houston, Dallas, San Antonio, Austin, El Paso, Fort Worth

Land area: 266,874 mi² (691,201 km²), including 4,959 mi² (12,843 km²) of inland water, but excluding 404 mi² (1,047 km²) of coastal water

✳ FLAG DATA ✳

- The state flag of Texas features a vertical blue stripe at the hoist with a large white star. The *fly* (the free end of a flag, farthest from the staff) features two horizontal stripes of white and red.

- The flag's width-to-length ratio is 2 to 3.

##

C4 ABOUT UTAH

Utah is a state in the Rocky Mountain region of the United States. Much of Utah is desert. The Rocky Mountains extend into the northeast corner of the state. The Great Salt Lake, in far northern Utah, is the largest natural lake in the western United States.

American Indians lived in present-day Utah when Mormons—that is, members of what is now called the Church of Jesus Christ of Latter-day Saints—became the region's first permanent white settlers in 1847. Utah became a U.S. territory in 1850. The world's first transcontinental railroad system was completed at Promontory in 1869. Many Mormons moved to Utah. Today, Salt Lake City, Utah, is the worldwide headquarters of the church.

About 85 percent of Utah's population is of European ancestry, chiefly English, German, Danish, or Irish. Hispanics make up about 9 percent of the population. About 70 percent of Utah's people are Mormons.

Most of Utah's economy is made up of service industries. Utah also has rich mineral deposits. The state's leading mineral products are petroleum, copper, and coal. Utah's national parks, ski resorts, and breathtaking scenery attract many tourists.

ABOUT THE FLAG OF UTAH

The design of Utah's seal was adopted in 1850 by the Territory of Utah. A new seal, designed by artist Harry Edwards, was adopted in 1896 when Utah became a state. Edwards added a bald eagle and crossed U.S. flags to indicate the protection of the United States and Utah's loyalty to the nation. The date 1847 on the seal refers to the date the Mormons came to Utah. The date 1896 on the seal refers to the year that Utah joined the Union. Also included on the seal are the word *Industry* and a beehive. Deseret, part of the Mormon settlers' name for the territory, means *honey bee*. On either side of the beehive are sego lilies, the state flower. The lilies are said to be symbols of peace. They also refer to a time when early settlers were forced to eat the bulbs of the lily to survive.

In March 1911, Utah adopted a flag proposed by the state's Daughters of the American Revolution group. The official design featured the state seal in white in the banner's center. However, another flag with the seal in full color was presented to the warship U.S.S. *Utah*. This design was so popular that it was made official in a new flag law on March 11, 1913. Utah's flag has not been altered since that time.

STATE DATA

Popular name: The Beehive State

Capital: Salt Lake City

Song: "Utah, We Love Thee"

Motto: *Industry*

Bird: California sea gull

Flower: Sego lily

Tree: Blue spruce

Executive: Governor

Largest cities: Salt Lake City, West Valley City, Provo, Sandy, Orem, Ogden

Land area: 84,905 mi² (216,902 km²), including 2,736 mi² (7,086 km²) of inland water

✸ FLAG DATA ✸

- The state flag of Utah features a dark blue *field* (background) with the state seal in the center.

- The most common width-to-length ratios for the flag are 2 to 3, 3 to 5, and 5 to 8.

ABOUT VERMONT

Vermont is a state in the New England region of the United States. Its forested Green Mountains make Vermont one of the most scenic states. Forests cover about 80 percent of Vermont.

Indians lived in the region that is now Vermont when the first European explorers arrived there in the early 1600's. Vermont's first permanent white settlement was established in what is now Brattleboro. The region became a British colony. A group of Vermont soldiers called the Green Mountain Boys fought the British both before and during the Revolutionary War in America (1775–1783). Led by Ethan Allen (1738–1789), they gained fame for their capture of Fort Ticonderoga from the British in 1775.

Vermont is the most rural of the U.S. states. More than 60 percent of its people live in rural areas. It also has fewer people than any other U.S. state except Wyoming. People of English, Irish, French, German, and French-Canadian descent make up Vermont's largest population groups.

Service industries employ about three-quarters of Vermont's workers. Tourism is also important to the state's economy. The state is among the leading maple syrup-producing states.

ABOUT THE FLAG OF VERMONT

Vermont's first state flag was adopted in 1803. The banner was used for the state's militia. It had 17 white stars in its blue *canton* (the upper corner of a flag, next to the staff) and 17 stripes, corresponding to the number of states in the Union in 1804. The name of the state was shown at the top of the flag.

The second Vermont state flag was adopted in 1837. It showed the state seal on a white star in a blue canton. The rest of the flag was made up of 13 red and white horizontal stripes.

In 1923, Vermont adopted its current flag. The banner resembles nearly half of all state flags in having a state emblem centered on a blue *field* (background). The flag features the 1821 Vermont coat of arms, which is based on the state seal. The coat of arms shows a scene with mountains in the background, a large pine tree in the foreground, sheaves of grain, and a cow. The motto *Freedom and Unity*, the name of the state, two pine branches, and the head of a deer complete the design.

STATE DATA

Popular name: The Green Mountain State

Capital: Montpelier

Song: "Hail, Vermont"

Motto: *Freedom and Unity*

Bird: Hermit thrush

Flower: Red clover

Tree: Sugar maple

Executive: Governor

Largest cities: Burlington, Essex, Rutland, Colchester, South Burlington, Bennington

Land area: 9,615 mi² (24,903 km²), including 366 mi² (947 km²) of inland water

✳ FLAG DATA ✳

- The state flag of Vermont features a dark blue field with a central coat of arms.

- The most common width-to-length ratios for the flag are 2 to 3, 3 to 5, and 5 to 8.

C4 ABOUT VIRGINIA

Virginia is a Southern state on the Atlantic Coast of the United States. Much of central Virginia is a rolling plain. In the southwest of the state is a high, rugged plateau, and mountains rise in the west.

Several Indian groups occupied what is now Virginia when Europeans arrived. In 1607, the first permanent English settlement in America was founded at Jamestown. Despite Virginia's long-standing status as a British colony, such Virginians as Patrick Henry (1736–1799) and Thomas Jefferson (1743–1826) were among the leading statesmen who voiced complaints over British policies. The decisive American victory in the Revolutionary War (1775–1783) took place at Yorktown in 1781. During the American Civil War (1861–1865), the capital of the southern Confederacy was at Richmond. The Civil War officially ended with the surrender of Confederate forces at Appomattox.

People of German, English, and Irish descent make up much of Virginia's white population. About 20 percent of the state's people are African Americans, and about 5 percent are Hispanics.

Service industries make up the largest part of Virginia's economy. The state's economy was once based on tobacco, and even today it is Virginia's most valuable cash crop. Virginia's beautiful scenery and historic sites attract millions of tourists every year.

ABOUT THE FLAG OF VIRGINIA

Some historians believe that Virginia statesman George Wythe created Virginia's first state seal, which was adopted in 1776. He probably based his design on a book about Roman artifacts by Joseph Spence. Wythe's design was made in two sizes and had different designs on the *obverse* (the side of a coin, medal, flag, or the like, that features the principal design) and *reverse* (back side). The reverse showed women who symbolized liberty, eternity, and agriculture.

The design on the obverse of the seal now appears on Virginia's state flag. It features a woman representing virtue dressed as an Amazon. (The Amazons were a tribe of women warriors in Greek mythology.) The woman on the seal wears a helmet and holds a spear and sword above the motto *Sic Semper Tyrannis* (Thus Always to Tyrants). She is standing on the figure of a man whose crown has fallen from his head. He holds a whip and chain. The scene recalls a popular theme of the time, victory over unjust governments.

On April 30, 1861, the legislature placed the emblem on a blue *field* (background) as the official state flag.

STATE DATA

Popular name: Old Dominion

Capital: Richmond

Motto: *Sic Semper Tyrannis* (Thus Always to Tyrants)

Bird: Cardinal

Flower: Flowering dogwood

Tree: Flowering dogwood

Executive: Governor

Largest cities: Virginia Beach, Norfolk, Chesapeake, Richmond, Arlington, Newport News

Land area: 40,598 mi^2 (105,149 km^2), including 1,000 mi^2 (2,591 km^2) of inland water, but excluding 1,728 mi^2 (4,476 km^2) of coastal water

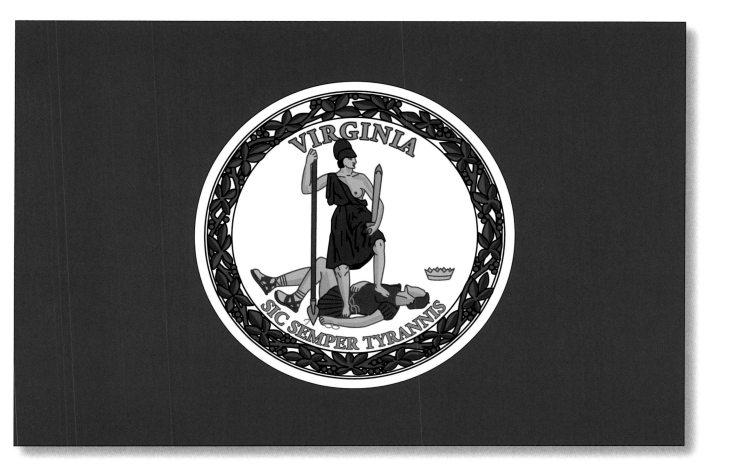

✹ FLAG DATA ✹

- The state flag of Virginia features a dark blue field with the obverse side of the state seal in the center.

- The most common width-to-length ratios for the flag are 2 to 3, 3 to 5, and 5 to 8.

C4 ABOUT WASHINGTON

Washington is a state in the Pacific Coast region of the United States. Mountain ranges in the state include the Olympic Mountains, in the northwest; the Cascades, in central Washington; and the Rocky Mountains, in the northeast corner. Washington's landscape is famous for its beauty and variety. The state has large areas of thick forests, especially on the western slopes of the Cascades. Temperate rain forests grow on the Olympic Peninsula.

Many Indian tribes lived in the Washington region before Europeans arrived. British and American explorers claimed the region that is now Washington for their respective countries in the late 1700's and early 1800's. British and American fur traders both operated in the region. Washington became a state in the 1880's, soon after the completion of a railroad connection with the East.

Washington's largest population groups include people with German, English, Irish, Norwegian, French, Swedish, American Indian, Scottish, and Dutch ancestry. A number of Hispanics, Asian Americans, and African Americans also live in the state.

Community, business, and personal services, chiefly the creation of computer software, is the state's top economic activity. Timber is Washington's most valuable agricultural product, and Washington is one of the top U.S. timber-producing states.

ABOUT THE FLAG OF WASHINGTON

In the 1800's, the territorial seal of Washington showed a detailed scene with a woman in the foreground symbolizing hope, surrounded by a log cabin, wagon, and fir forest. That design was replaced when Washington became a state in 1889. That year, a design with the likeness of George Washington, the date of admission to the Union, and the name of the state was adopted as the state seal. The seal was created by brothers Charles and Grant Talcott, who were both jewelers.

In 1915, members of the Daughters of the American Revolution chose a green *field* (background) for the flag of the *Evergreen State* and placed a bust of President George Washington in the center. In 1920, the training ship owned by the Washington State Nautical School flew a similar flag.

The green state flag adopted by the state legislature in 1923 featured the state seal in its center. Originally, the flag could be decorated with green fringe. In 1925, however, the law was changed to alter the fringe color to gold. In 1967, the flag's design was more precisely defined by state law. That law requires the seal to appear correctly on both sides of the flag. Washington is the only U.S. state to have a banner with a green field.

STATE DATA

Popular name: The Evergreen State

Capital: Olympia

Song: "Washington, My Home"

Motto: *Alki* (an Indian word for Bye and Bye)

Bird: Willow goldfinch

Flower: Coast rhododendron

Tree: Western hemlock

Executive: Governor

Largest cities: Seattle, Spokane, Tacoma, Vancouver, Bellevue, Everett

Land area: 68,126 mi^2 (176,446 km^2), including 1,545 mi^2 (4,001 km^2) of inland water, but excluding 2,511 mi^2 (6,503 km^2) of coastal water

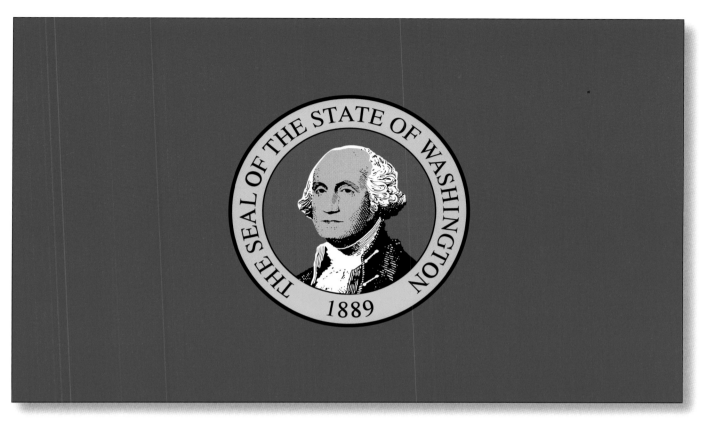

☀ FLAG DATA ☀

- The state flag of Washington features a green field with the state seal in the center.

- The most common width-to-length ratios for the flag are 2 to 3, 3 to 5, and 5 to 8.

C4 ABOUT WASHINGTON, D.C.

The D.C. in Washington, D.C., stands for District of Columbia. The District of Columbia is an area of 68 square miles (177 square kilometers) in the eastern United States. The U.S. capital, Washington, covers the entire district. While not a state, the District of Columbia shares some of the characteristics of a U.S. state. For example, Washington, D.C. is alloted three electors on the Electoral College, the body that elects the U.S. president. Further, Washington, D.C. is represented by a delegate in the U.S. House of Representatives.

The district lies on the northern bank of the Potomac River. The land rises gently to a series of hills to the north.

Nacotchtank Indians lived along the Potomac when Captain John Smith (1580?–1631) of the Jamestown Colony (Virginia) explored the area in 1608. The first U.S. president, George Washington (1732–1799), chose the district as the site of the federal capital in 1790 and commissioned Pierre Charles L'Enfant (1754–1825), a French engineer, to create the city's plan. The federal government moved to the district from Philadelphia in 1800.

More than 50 percent of district residents are African Americans. About 30 percent are white, and most of the remainder are Hispanic, Asian, or American Indian.

The economy is based almost entirely on activities of the federal government and tourism. Millions of tourists annually visit the district for its historic sites, monuments, and museums.

ABOUT THE FLAG OF WASHINGTON, D.C.

After World War I (1914–1918), a number of designs were proposed for a flag to represent Washington, D.C. In February 1924, a flag design was submitted to the *Evening Star* newspaper by graphics designer Charles Dunn. Dunn's banner had a white *field* (background) with two horizontal red stripes and three blue, five-pointed stars. Dunn had based his design on the personal coat of arms of George Washington. Washington's arms were similar but showed red *rowels* (the sharp pointed disks at the end of spurs) instead of blue stars. The Washington family arms date to the 1500's in Sulgrave, England. However, the intended symbolism of the design and colors is unknown.

In 1938, the U.S. Congress established a special flag commission to select a banner for the district. The commission considered a version of the Dunn flag with red stars instead of blue. It also considered a more complex design created by the Daughters of the American Revolution. The group finally selected the "Washington arms" flag, as Dunn's design was known.

The flag was first flown in October 1938. It was not, however, widely used in the district for another 20 years. It has been suggested that the three red stars symbolize the three commissioners who once ran the district. This claim, however, cannot be documented.

DISTRICT DATA

Executive: Mayor

Land area: 68 mi² (177 km²)

✷ FLAG DATA ✷

- The flag of Washington, D.C. features a white field with two horizontal red stripes of equal width and three red stars above the stripes.

- The most common width-to-length ratios for the flag are 2 to 3, 3 to 5, and 5 to 8.

C4 ABOUT WEST VIRGINIA

West Virginia is a Southern state of the United States. Located in the Appalachian Highlands, the state has some of the nation's most rugged land. The eastern and central regions of West Virginia are covered by mountain chains, and the region west of the mountains is characterized by steep and rolling hills and narrow valleys.

In the 1700's, West Virginia was part of Virginia. Western Virginians disagreed with eastern Virginians on many issues, including slavery, which was generally opposed by western Virginians. During the Civil War (1861–1865), when Virginia became part of the Confederacy, western Virginia broke apart from the rest of Virginia and remained loyal to the Union. West Virginia became a separate state in 1863.

Almost all of West Virginia's people were born in the United States. Many have German, Irish, Scots-Irish, English, African, or American Indian ancestry.

West Virginia is one of the top U.S. coal-producing states. Among West Virginia's other mined products, natural gas is the most important. Chemicals are by far West Virginia's most valuable manufactured product.

ABOUT THE FLAG OF WEST VIRGINIA

West Virginia's coat of arms is encircled by a wreath of big laurel (*Rhododendron maximum*), which was made the state flower in 1903. The following year, the big laurel was featured on the *obverse* (the side of a coin, medal, flag, or the like, that features the principal design) of a flag made to represent West Virginia at the Louisiana Purchase Exposition in St. Louis, Missouri. That flag was white with a red and blue border. The state coat of arms appeared on the reverse side. The arms are part of the state seal, designed by Joseph H. D. Debar and adopted in 1863. On Feb. 24, 1905, West Virginia's legislature recognized the 1904 banner as the state's flag. In February 1907, however, the legislature switched the state arms to the front of the flag and placed the flower on the *reverse* (back) side. A scroll with the phrase *State of West Virginia* was added beneath the arms. In 1929, the scroll was moved above the arms.

The farmer and the miner in the coat of arms stand on either side of a rock that bears the date that West Virginia became a state, June 20, 1863. The cap of liberty and crossed rifles in the foreground recall the Latin motto that appears below, *Montani Semper Liberi* (Mountaineers Are Always Free). The motto is a reminder that West Virginia was created when the mountainous areas of western Virginia seceded from the rest of the state after slave-holding Virginia became part of the Confederacy in 1861.

In 1929, the legislature approved the present form of the flag. Because of the expense and difficulty of making a double-sided flag, the legislature voted to show the same symbol on both sides. The symbol chosen was the coat of arms framed by branches of big laurel.

STATE DATA

Popular name: The Mountain State

Capital: Charleston

Song: "The West Virginia Hills" (one of three state songs)

Motto: *Montani Semper Liberi* (Mountaineers Are Always Free)

Bird: Cardinal

Flower: Rhododendron

Tree: Sugar maple

Executive: Governor

Largest cities: Charleston, Huntington, Parkersburg, Wheeling, Morgantown, Weirton

Land area: 24,231 mi^2 (62,759 km^2), including 145 mi^2 (375 km^2) of inland water

☀ FLAG DATA ☀

- The state flag of West Virginia features a white *field* (background) bordered in blue with a coat of arms in the center.

- The flag's width-to-length ratio is 10 to 19.

ABOUT WISCONSIN

Wisconsin is a state in the Midwestern region of the United States. Most of northern Wisconsin is covered by heavily forested hills. The central part of the state is a flat plain. Western Wisconsin has steep slopes and winding ridges. In the east, there are rolling plains and limestone ridges. The state borders on the Great Lakes of Michigan and Superior.

French explorers were the first Europeans to arrive in what is now Wisconsin, in the 1600's. The British gained control of the region in 1763. It became a U.S. territory after the Revolutionary War (1775–1783). After statehood in 1848, Wisconsin developed a reputation as one of the most progressive U.S. states.

About 97 percent of Wisconsin's people were born in the United States. More than half are of German descent. Other large population groups there include people with Irish, Polish, English, and African American ancestry.

Wisconsin is one of the top states in the production of machinery, food products, and paper products. Wisconsin has long been famous for its dairy products. It leads the states in the production of milk, butter, cheese, ice cream, and other milk products. Corn is the state's most important crop.

ABOUT THE FLAG OF WISCONSIN

On March 25, 1863, Wisconsin adopted a blue flag with the state's coat of arms on the *obverse* (the side of a coin, medal, flag, or the like, that features the principal design) side and the national arms on the *reverse* (back side). When the flag was readopted in April 1913, the Wisconsin arms appeared on both sides. The flag's design was altered in 1979. The name of the state was added above the arms, and the date it joined the Union (1848) was added below.

In its present form, the coat of arms dates from 1881, although the basic design had been created 30 years earlier. The U.S. motto *E Pluribus Unum* (One Out of Many) appears in the center, along with a shield. They are surrounded by symbols of occupations that were common in the 1800's—farming, mining, manufacturing, and shipping. A miner and sailor serve as the shield's *supporters*, the figures on either side of an emblem. Above the shield is a badger, referring to the state's nickname, *The Badger State*. Wisconsin earned this nickname because early miners either lived in mine shafts or dug burrowlike huts that resembled badger holes. Above the badger is a scroll with the state's motto, *Forward*. Below the shield are a cornucopia and a pyramid of lead ingots.

STATE DATA

Popular name: The Badger State

Capital: Madison

Song: "On, Wisconsin!"

Motto: *Forward*

Bird: Robin

Flower: Wood violet

Tree: Sugar maple

Executive: Governor

Largest cities: Milwaukee, Madison, Green Bay, Kenosha, Racine, Appleton

Land area: 56,145 mi^2 (145,414 km^2), including 1,831 mi^2 (4,741 km^2) of inland water, but excluding 9,355 mi^2 (24,229 km^2) of Great Lakes water

- The state flag features a dark blue *field* (background) with a central coat of arms, the name of the state, and the date 1848.

- The flag's width-to-length ratio is 2 to 3.

ABOUT WYOMING

Wyoming is a state in the Rocky Mountain region of the United States. Several ranges of the Rocky Mountains dominate much of the state's landscape, but not all of Wyoming is mountainous. Between the mountain ranges are broad, flat, treeless basins. Eastern Wyoming, part of the Great Plains, is a flat, dry plain.

Wyoming's first inhabitants were Indians. The region that is now Wyoming joined the United States as part of the Louisiana Purchase in 1803. In the mid-1800's, with the discovery of oil and gold and the completion of the transcontinental railroad through the area, Wyoming grew. In 1872, the country's first national park, Yellowstone, was created in northwestern Wyoming.

Wyoming has fewer people than any other state. About 89 percent of Wyoming's people are non-Hispanic whites, about 6 percent are of Hispanic descent, and about 2 percent are American Indian.

Service industries make up the largest component of Wyoming's economy. However, mining makes up a larger part of the economy of Wyoming than that of any other state. Wyoming's most important product is coal. Natural gas and petroleum are also a key part of Wyoming's economy. Wyoming's chief agricultural activity is cattle ranching. It is one of the top sheep- and wool-producing states.

ABOUT THE FLAG OF WYOMING

Wyoming's seal was adopted by the state legislature in 1893. It includes the state motto, *Equal Rights*. Wyoming was the first state to grant unrestricted civil and politi-cal rights to women. The figures of the miner and cowboy on either side of the woman in the seal's center refer to two important industries of the state. Four of Wyoming's major industries are mentioned in the ribbon wrapped around the two pillars, which bears the words *Livestock, Mines, Grain, Oil.* The seal also includes an American eagle over a shield and star bearing the number 44. The number refers to Wyoming's status as the 44th state to join the Union. The design of the seal is completed by the dates 1869 and 1890, representing the years Wyoming became a territory and a state.

In 1916, 37 proposals were submitted in a flag design competition sponsored by the Daughters of the American Revolution. The winning designer was Verna Keays from Buffalo, Wyoming. Her flag featured the national colors, the white silhouette of a bison, and the Wyoming state seal. The seal appeared on the flank, or side, of the bison, referring to the Western tradition of branding animals. On Jan. 31, 1917, the legislature adopted the flag that Keays designed. The white is said to stand for purity and uprightness. The blue represents the sky and mountains as well as fidelity, justice, and virility, or strength. The red border symbolizes both the blood shed by early pioneers and the original Native American people who lived in the state.

STATE DATA

Popular name: The Equality State

Capital: Cheyenne

Song: "Wyoming"

Motto: *Equal Rights*

Bird: Meadowlark

Flower: Indian paintbrush

Tree: Cottonwood

Executive: Governor

Largest cities: Cheyenne, Casper, Laramie, Gillette, Rock Springs, Sheridan

Land area: 97,818 mi^2 (253,349 km^2), including 714 mi^2 (1,848 km^2) of inland water

✳ FLAG DATA ✳

- The state flag of Wyoming features a dark blue *field* (background) bordered by white and red. In the center is the white silhouette of a bison bearing the state seal.

- The flag's width-to-length ratio is 7 to 10.

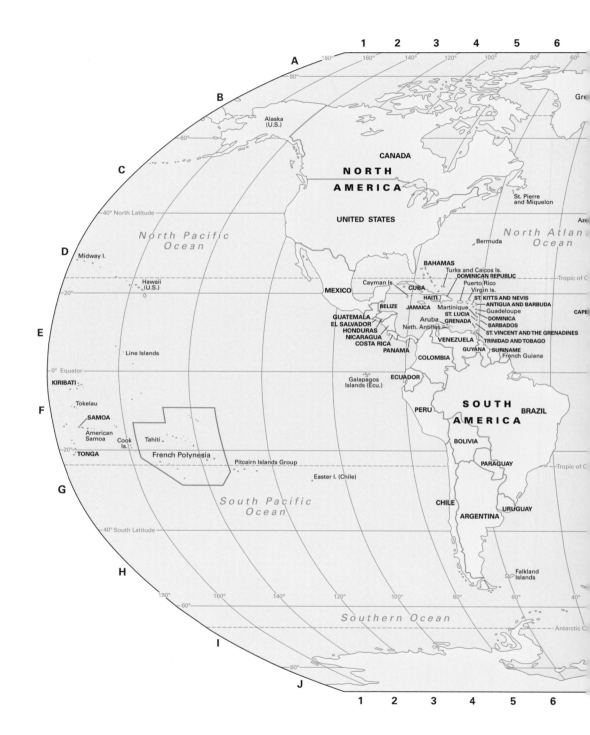

	1	2	3	4	5	6

A 180° 160° 140° 120° 100° 80° 60°

B 80°

Gre

Alaska
(U.S.)

60°

C CANADA

**NORTH
AMERICA**

St. Pierre
and Miquelon

40° North Latitude

*North Pacific
Ocean*

UNITED STATES

*North Atlan
Ocean*

Aze

D Midway I.

Bermuda

BAHAMAS

Turks and Caicos Is.
DOMINICAN REPUBLIC

Tropic of C

Hawaii
(U.S.)

20°

Cayman Is. CUBA

Puerto Rico
Virgin Is.

MEXICO

HAITI

ST. KITTS AND NEVIS
ANTIGUA AND BARBUDA

CAPE

BELIZE

Martinique

JAMAICA

Guadeloupe

GUATEMALA

ST. LUCIA

DOMINICA

EL SALVADOR

Aruba

GRENADA

BARBADOS

HONDURAS

Neth. Antilles

ST. VINCENT AND THE GRENADINES

E NICARAGUA

VENEZUELA

TRINIDAD AND TOBAGO

COSTA RICA

GUYANA

SURINAME

PANAMA

French Guiana

COLOMBIA

Line Islands

ECUADOR

0° Equator

Galapagos
Islands (Ecu.)

KIRIBATI

Tokelau

**SOUTH
AMERICA**

F SAMOA

PERU

BRAZIL

American
Samoa

Cook
Is.

Tahiti

BOLIVIA

20°

TONGA

French Polynesia

Pitcairn Islands Group

Tropic of C

PARAGUAY

Easter I. (Chile)

G

*South Pacific
Ocean*

CHILE

URUGUAY

ARGENTINA

40° South Latitude

H

Falkland
Islands

180° 160° 140° 120° 100° 80° 60° 40°

60°

Southern Ocean

Antarctic C

I

80°

J

	1	2	3	4	5	6